# The Journey
## 13 Steps in Discipleship

By Bill McDonald

# Dedication

*To my friend, my lover, my wife.*
*These three, are just one,*
*with whom I share life.*

# Endorsements

Bill's book, *The Journey*, is nothing less than a spiritual travel guide, taking his readers through the steps of the incredible faith journey called *discipleship*.

Seasoned saints as well as new believers will find his practical approach most refreshing.

—Mark Batterson
New York Times best-selling author of *The Circle Maker*
Lead Pastor of National Community Church

More than twenty years ago I stood with Bill McDonald in the Andes Mountains of Ecuador and committed to a lifetime of partnering to accomplish our part of the Great Commission. It has been a joy to see firsthand how Bill, as a pastor, apostle, missionary and visionary, has walked out his commitment to go into all the world and make disciples.

For Bill, discipleship has never been about working a program or developing a 7-step process of spiritual maturity. It has always been about a relationship with God and the people around him. Like very few in the world Bill has modeled for people of all backgrounds by simply conveying Jesus to them through scriptural truth and real-life applications. In his most recent book, *The Journey*, Bill gives an intimate and transparent look at what it takes to make disciples, by first of all being one. As you read through this book it will challenge and excite you with the realization that the *journey* is possible and essential for each one of us. I am thankful for the insights throughout this book and excited for generations of people who are asking God to take them on this *journey* of discipleship for His glory and the changing of lives for eternity.

—Mark Lehmann
Pastor, Cornerstone Church
Bowie, Maryland

Bill's thirty-year missionary experience has taught him the simplicity of Jesus' instructions in how to go and make disciples. Why spend time and money on programs when Jesus made it so easy? This book will help many as it encourages us to share our stories – the greatest story ever told!

—Jean Eason
Tutors for Christ Ministry

Bill and Connie McDonald have lived the life of discipleship like few others in our modern era. Grafting and weaving personal testimonials, discipling anecdotes, and years of Andean-Incan history and heritage shared with the Ecuadorian and Amazonian peoples brings a beautiful insight to the scriptural analogies offered in this values-rich manuscript. From my first-encounter when we met in the early 1980's to now over twenty expeditions throughout Ecuador and the Amazonia Region with Bill and Connie McDonald, I have witnessed first-hand this apostolic, charismatic, and genuinely gracious man of prayer and faith believe in people, bring hope to the hopeless, and make paths to the cross brighter and wider for those to trek. His "Journey" and his devotion and personal encounter with a living God brings a fresh fire that awakens the soul!

—Joseph S. Girdler, M.Div.
Superintendent Kentucky Assemblies of God

What an excellent book Bill has written on discipleship and yet, it's more than a book, it's a challenge to all of us who want to make a difference for the cause of Christ on this planet.

Reading, practicing, and sharing the principles found in *The Journey* is a tremendous vehicle to carry out the last command of Jesus to His followers and live a life of significance.

—Frankie Powell
Pastor/Evangelist

I served as a missionary to Latin America for 20 years with Bill McDonald, and he is one of my personal heroes. His big, bold faith, personal integrity, ministerial creativity, and persistence in charity provide a model that anyone would be wise to follow. How wonderful that he has codified his wisdom for us in *The Journey*!

—Joseph Castleberry, Ed. D, President, Northwest University and author of *Forty Days of Christmas*

I am a missionary because I long to go to my eternal home and I learn from Matthew 24:14 the shortest way home involves journeying to the nations with the gospel. Bill McDonald, with humor, humility, and history, gives practical discipleship device on how to journey home - from wherever you temporarily reside. *The Journey* elegantly and compellingly centers discipleship on the glory of God through simple and practical obedience. If you are motivated by the glory of God among all peoples and if you are determined to do the hands-on practical things daily discipleship demands – then you will benefit from this book as much as I have.

—Dick Brogden
Live Dead Founder, Cairo, Egypt

# Contents

Forewords                                          11
The Text: Luke 10:1-9                              13
Preface                                            15
A Word about S.T.O.P.                              21

**Part One – Plan the Plan**                       **23**
1. Appointed – Prevailing Purpose                  25
2. Two – Community Caravan                          39
3. Ask – Poignant Petition                         51

**Part Two – Step the Step**                       **65**
4. Go – Motivated Movement                          67
5. Wolves – Appreciated Anguish                     77

**Part Three – Don't the Don'ts**                  **91**
6. Purse – Cashless Capital                          93
7. Sandals – Sticky Stops                          107
8. Greet – Disastrous Distractions                 117

**Part Four – Leap the Leaps**                    **127**
9.  Enter – Daunting Doors                         129
10. Peace – Likeable Links                         141
11. Eat – Meaningful Meals                         153

**Part Five – Enjoy the Joy**                     **165**
12. Heal – Therapeutic Theology                    167
13. Tell – Practical Proclamation                  181

Conclusion                                         193

Appendix A - Questionnaire Checklist          197
Appendix B - How to Prepare Your Story        199
Appendix C - A Word about Mentoring           201

Acknowledgements                              205
Contact Us                                    207

# FOREWORD

An ancient proverb says, "The journey of a thousand miles begins with a single step." Bill and Connie have been on quite a journey. The road map has not always been clear, but their Guide has never failed them. Their journey has taken them from pulsating cities to perilous jungles. They have experienced breathtaking views from the mountaintop and trudged their way through the valley. Wherever they have gone, their faithfulness and obedience to the Lord, their Guide, has provided a sure pathway. They are people of great faith and character, and their story will inspire and encourage everyone who journeys with them.

—Greg Mundis
Executive Director,
Assemblies of God World Missions

# FOREWORD

This book by Bill McDonald is for everyone that intends to walk the Journey with Jesus. My wife and I have known Bill and Connie for many years and we are aware of their journey. What he says in his book he has practiced for the 30 years since we met them. Bill reminds us of 13 valuable truths, taken from the passage in Luke 10. If lived out in our lives, we will become faithful disciples and disciple-makers. While Bill and Connie would be considered great leaders, deeply spiritual and respected missionaries, I appreciated his intense desire to know God more and to reveal His glory to everyone that the Lord brings into our lives. Today, as he leads an important ministry in Cuenca, Ecuador with a national and international reach, you will see Bill and Connie living by these 13 truths that have shaped them on their journey all these years. I encourage you to study prayerfully these truths and apply them to your life as a fellow Jesus follower on the Journey.

—David A. Ellis
Regional Director, Latin America Caribbean
Assemblies of God World Missions

# The Text
## Luke 10:1-9

After this, the Lord appointed 72 others and sent them two by two ahead of Him to every town and place where He was about to go. He told them, "The harvest is plentiful, but the workers are few. Ask the Lord of the harvest, therefore, to send out workers into His harvest field. Go! I am sending you out like lambs among wolves. Do not take a purse or bag or sandals; and do not greet anyone on the road.

"When you enter a house, first say, 'Peace to this house.' If someone who promotes peace is there, your peace will rest on them; if not, it will return to you. Stay there, eating and drinking whatever they give you, for the worker deserves his wages. Do not move around from house to house.

"When you enter a town and are welcomed, eat what is offered to you. Heal the sick who are there and tell them, 'The kingdom of God has come near to you.'

# PREFACE

I am as proud, carnal, selfish, and egotistical as anyone I know. And worst, when I pull off a seemingly humble move, I am incredibly proud of my own humility! I can most definitely identify with the apostle Paul's words, "What a wretched man I am! Who will rescue me from this body that is subject to death? Thanks be to God, who delivers me through Jesus Christ our Lord!" (Romans 7:24-25). But if I know my heart, I am a lover of Christ, I love His Word, and I am bent on knowing Him. I identify completely with Brennan Manning when he writes, "My deepest awareness of myself is that I am deeply loved by Jesus Christ, and I have done nothing to earn it or deserve it."[1]

As I dig deeper into His Word, I become more persuaded I have done a lot of things wrong. At times, I would like a do-over, but obviously that is not going to happen. As my friend and pastor Frankie says, "It is difficult for a man to change when his livelihood depends on him not changing."[2] The things I write about in this book seem to fly in the face of everything I have done and am presently doing.

I talk about a luggage-less *journey*, and we are raising up a multimillion dollar television enterprise. I talk about communities of personal interaction, yet I have been part of founding and constructing megachurches. I talk about the errors of institutionalism, yet I am or have been CEO, president, general manager, and board member of various organizations.

---

[1] Manning, Brennan. *The Ragamuffin Gospel: Good News for the Bedraggled, Beat-Up, and Burnt Out* (pp. 25-26). The Crown Publishing Group.
2 Paraphrase from Upton Sinclair's, I, Candidate for Governor: And How I Got *Licked,* 1935. Original quote is, "It is difficult to get a man to understand something, when his salary depends upon his not understanding it!"

I talk about missions being more about staying than going, yet I'm a Gold AAdvantage member. So ... I am a long way from working all this out. I have decided, however, that the words directed to Joshua from the Lord himself will become words for my own destiny, "Dude, you are old. But hey, there is still a lot for you to accomplish!" (obviously, my paraphrase of Joshua 13:1).

So, I continue to ask questions like what is true discipleship? Who does a person need to be, and what does a person need to do to make disciples? Has the Church made *going* way more complicated than Jesus ever intended it to be? Have we missed an enormous opportunity to lead untold people to faith in Jesus Christ because we've got the going — the discipleship *journey* — wrong?

Such questions grew even louder in my mind eight years ago when I was diagnosed with an extremely aggressive prostate cancer. As I battled it, Jesus grabbed my full and undivided attention.

Like anyone facing such a foe, I found strength in leaning on the Lord through prayer, learned as much as I could about my sickness, and hoped for the best while expecting the worst. During that time, I also found much fuel for my faith in the New Testament. I read and reread it several times, as if encountering the text for the first time, devouring it over and over again in short order.

Two observations stood out most to this seasoned lover of Scripture. One, there are many commands in the New Testament that we, as followers of Jesus, don't keep.

And two, many of our behaviors and activities have no biblical basis. Some would consider this to be the greatest crisis of the Church today: "A regular and perverse ability to make things work that are not and should not be working. We learn to adjust to things that we should alter. We learn to be okay with things we should be confronting. We learn how to avoid things we should be facing."[3]

As I thought through this, I also considered that every postmodern society wrestles with its own social tradition. And if that is the case, maybe it's time for Christians to understand what it means to be the Church in this new cultural context.[4] If the Church does rise to the occasion, I believe that She will look for a new reformation rather than another awakening.

I pushed through the Scriptures again and did so as a novice learner. I didn't look for reasons, answers, purpose, or strength for my cancer. My question focused more on the possibility of a more efficient way to take this *journey* of discipleship. And by God's grace during this season of study, I landed on some critical thoughts that spawned one of the most transformative periods of my life, especially when I landed on Luke 10.

> After this, the Lord appointed 72 others and sent them two by two ahead of Him to every town and place where He was about to go. He told them, "The harvest is plentiful, but the workers are few. Ask the Lord of the harvest, therefore, to send out workers into His harvest field. Go! I am sending you out like lambs among wolves. Do not take a purse or bag or sandals; and do not greet anyone on the road.

---

[3] Tripp, Paul David. *Dangerous Calling: Confronting the Unique Challenges of Pastoral Ministry* (p. 59). Crossway.
[4] Sweet, Leonard. *Soul Tsunami: Sink or Swim in New Millennium Culture* (pp. 227-229). Zondervan.

"When you enter a house, first say, 'Peace to this house.' If someone who promotes peace is there, your peace will rest on them; if not, it will return to you. Stay there, eating and drinking whatever they give you, for the worker deserves his wages. Do not move around from house to house.

"When you enter a town and are welcomed, eat what is offered to you. Heal the sick who are there and tell them, 'The kingdom of God has come near to you.'"[5]

Specifically, 13 words jumped off the page and challenged my concept of the *journey*.

*appointed, two, ask,*
*go, wolves,*
*purse, sandals, greet,*
*enter, peace, eat,*
*heal, and tell*

This seemingly run-of-the-mill collection of nouns and verbs transformed my thinking, redefining the way I viewed my place in the world, what it means to go, and how I would spend my remaining days on earth. Standing alone, these words aren't too exciting. But throw them under the light of discipleship and evangelism, and suddenly these little morsels become full banquets filled with life-changing — even eternal — implications that demand a change of course in the way we minister and live. For Jesus' words are much more than poetic; they are nothing less than strategic.

So here is the motivation behind this study. As I wrote earlier, maybe, just maybe, there is another way — a more effective way — of doing Christian life, ministry and missions. Perhaps

---

[5] Luke 10:1-11, emphasis added.

the *journey* Jesus laid out for His disciples 2,000 years ago in Luke 10 is just as applicable and practical for His disciples today. And maybe the *journey* is more than a suggestion; it's a mandate.

Now I can see there were times when I found more contentment in constructing buildings and racking up numbers in the pews than in building the kingdom of God by going and making disciples as Jesus told His disciples to do in Matthew 28:19.

Please understand, I have no reason or desire to throw stones at massive projects, traditional churches, or crowd-gathering campaigns. After all, I am a product of such activities, and grateful that God used them, in part, to reach me.

However, I am convinced now, more than ever, that Jesus has given His church a map for an incredible *journey*. I see the New Testament as more than doctrines and dogmas; it is also a blueprint for a life-transforming and Kingdom-building *journey* for His disciples. This design is a call to action for you and me — and the Church, hopefully — to rely on the basics of evangelism, telling us to go and make disciples. That's what life as a follower of Jesus is all about. We are to live a *journey* of discipleship.

Today, there are 2.3 billion living Christians[6] (whom I will refer to as followers of Jesus or a similar derivative throughout this book). Millions of them have access to some of the greatest technology, financial resources, infrastructure, transportation, logistics, and talent to ensure that everyone on earth is adequately presented with the gospel of Jesus.

---

[6] Hackett, Conrad. *Christians remain world's largest religious group, but they are declining in Europe*, April 5, 2017, Pew Research Center.

The problem is that there are still hundreds of millions of people who have never heard the gospel. That's unacceptable! It's also precisely why all of us who call ourselves followers of Jesus need to refocus our objectives on the *journey* of going and making disciples, no matter the costs.

From little to large — in homes, tents, storefronts, and major construction projects — my wife, Connie, and I have planted churches in major cities, rural communities, and jungle villages. We've practiced friendship evangelism, held home groups, led Bible schools, directed multimillion dollar capital campaigns, founded a television station, and held faith-based conferences and workshops. This all occurred in the name of leading people into a relationship with Jesus. But four decades into it, there is more need for discipleship today than the day we started.

Tragically, there are many more people yet to call Jesus "Lord" in the very places we have spent a lifetime of service. I can't help but think that if we employed the simple strategies that Jesus Christ gave in Luke 10, we would become more efficient at building the kingdom of God. I believe this *journey* is for each of us and my prayer is that a study of His words will not only change the way you share your faith, but transform the lives of countless people with whom you come into contact.

For the *Journey*,

Bill

# A Word about S.T.O.P

A good book will engage our emotions, enslave our hearts, and employ our intellect, even if it is just for a moment. A few books, however, will not only engage, enslave, and employ, but will push deep into our souls to disrupt our plans, disturb our peace, and disorder our future, for a better cause. Francis Bacon wrote, "Some books should be tasted, some devoured, but only a few should be chewed and digested thoroughly."

Most definitely the words of Jesus should be chewed and digested thoroughly. In order to savor these morsels of 13 words and appreciate their applications, I have developed a S.T.O.P inductive method to aid the reader in the digestive process.

After each chapter, you will be challenged to ponder the Key Word again through a series of questions to bring about an applicable goal or action point. Then to bring the word to a relevant conclusion, you will have the opportunity to respond to four additional questions concerning your goals.

Are your goals:

**S** — Specific? Establish a goal that is not vague or general. For example, don't just set a goal of praying more. Set a specific time of prayer. In this way, you can quantifiably measure your progress.

**T** — Time Sensitive? Don't leave your goals open-ended. Set a time by which you hope to accomplish your goal. "I plan to be baptized before the end of the year," would be an example.

**O** — Obtainable? Make sure your goals are within reach.

**P** — Pertinent? It is important that your goals align with the material you are studying.

I do understand that this task will be somewhat laborious. However, I am sure the investment will bring much fruit and deep satisfaction.

# PART ONE
## *Plan the Plan*

Key words one, two and three: Appointed – Two – Ask

The first hundred or so times I read Luke 10, I failed to notice that the *journey* Jesus proposes has great structure to it. Like any good motivator and organizer, Jesus lays out a plan for His disciples. And the first phase of this *journey*, like most successful *journeys*, begins with a plan.

First, they are appointed. They understand the call.
Secondly, they are placed in a team. Teamwork.
Thirdly, they begin not by going, but by asking.

As you read these first three chapters, I hope you will start to question yourself. Do I understand my appointment? Who is on my team? Have I bathed my call and team in asking and prayer?

### Plans
Ponder them twice,
three times a better bet.
Four times may be wise,
tomorrow better yet.

Count the high cost,
weighing the price.
Consider possible loss and
seek good advice.

Completing all this,
you'll surely have seen
when plans go amiss,
new lessons are gleaned.
— W. E. M.

—

# 1

## Word One – Appointed
### *Prevailing Purpose*

Key word: Appointed – To assign officially, as for a position, responsibility.[7]

Key verse: "...the Lord appointed 72[8] others and sent them..." Luke 10:1

Key thought: The *journey*, as a disciple of Christ, is a call and appointment to serve specifically within the body of Christ. We should strive to decipher and exercise that gift. The overarching call, however, is to bring glory to God. The *journey* (not this book, but life) is all about His glory.

I had read this verse hundreds of times over my years of faith. But now, as if looking through special glasses that could

---

[7] Oxford Dictionaries.

[8] The number "12" was meaningful in choosing disciples, so we are predisposed to regard the number 72 as significant, too. According to Genesis 10, the number of the world's nations is 72. Seventy-two is also reckoned in 3 passages: Enoch 17:8; 18:23; 30:2 as the number of princes and languages in the world. And according to legend, 72 elders were commissioned to translate the law from Hebrew to Greek, a project undertaken to win renown throughout the whole world for the Jews and their God (Epistle of Aristeas 35–51). Accordingly, the appointment of the 72 can be understood as prefiguring the universal mission in Acts." Green, Joel B. *The Gospel of Luke* (Kindle Locations 10600-10606). Eerdmans Publishing Co.

bring formerly hidden sights into existence, the word appointed came alive. I asked myself a series of quick questions: Is this appointment for just the 72? Are just a few appointed? What is involved in that appointment? Am I appointed? If so, what is my assignment? Some of the answers I found surprised me. Maybe they will surprise you, too.

## Running with No Purpose

In 2 Samuel 18, King David waited to receive word from Ahimaaz, a running messenger, about the well-being of his son, Absalom. The king urgently asks the breathless courier, "How is my son, Absalom?" Sadly, the runner had no idea. He had run hard but had no message. "I don't know," he continued. "I just saw a crowd and I ran." "Stand back!" cried David. "A second runner, Cushi, is coming."

Ahimaaz ran well. The good athlete possessed better speed than Cushi, yet he didn't have a message. He had no idea about the purpose of his running. The takeaway from the story is obvious: it doesn't matter how well you can run; you must have a message when you arrive. Many of us are running hard. We want to serve, to give, and to go. But what is the goal? Why do we run?

## Puzzle Pieces

Connie and I love to work puzzles with our grandkids. But isn't it frustrating to finish a 1,000-piece puzzle only to discover one piece missing? You can show off your final work, and the picture may be awe-inspiring, but if one piece is missing, just *one* piece, the viewer's eyes will be drawn to that small empty space. The observer likely won't say, "You did a great job," but rather, "What did you do, lose one?"

The Scriptures assure us that *everyone* has a call to serve in a particular area, even if that individual has yet come to faith in Jesus Christ. As with a puzzle, a piece is either in the overall work, occupying its designated space, in the hands of the puzzler in search of that perfect place, or outside of the puzzle, in the box, or lost.

I see our Lord as the great puzzle builder. Each of us has a place in His grand scheme of space and time. Each one is appointed to her or his place in the puzzle, but won't fulfill its function until placed in its precise and predetermined destination. For each piece is appointed and chosen.[9] The Scriptures bear this out. Ephesians 2:10 declares, "For we are God's handiwork, created in Christ Jesus to do good works, which God prepared in advance for us to do." And Ephesians 4:7 says, "But to each one of us grace has been given as Christ apportioned it."

We should run as Cushi ran, maybe not as fast, but with purpose and determination, for we have an appointment, a call, and a message. "Finding that particular purpose for which we were born and answering the questions, *Why am I here on earth, what is my vocation?* is one of our most important assignments in life." [10]

Let me add that these positions (puzzle pieces) are not based on talent, ability, education, or job, because the Spirit calls and places as He wills. "There are different kinds of working, but in all of them and everyone it is the same God at work. Now to each one the manifestation of the Spirit is given for the common good" (1 Corinthians 12:6-7).

---

[9] Interestingly, this imaginary puzzle of human history would contain about 107,000,000,000 pieces. For that is the approximate number of people that have occupied a space on earth.
[10] Hinkey, Carmen. (2017-06-28) *Convinced of Your Calling, Following Jesus* blog.

---

## An Error

My concern, we have seen, is that the Church has erroneously identified the "appointed" as a particular "class" of individuals. For example, when I use the phrase, "called to ministry," what do you think? Ordination, full-time, pastor? This is where we have fallen into grave areas of, frankly, detrimental ignorance. Though there is an office of "pastors and elders" as well as other areas of leadership within the Church, the call is not exclusively for clergy. I understand why a church body would want to recognize, affirm, and honor the call on the life of an individual, but it is a mistake to elevate clergy above laity. The division into these classes is dangerous. (We'll dig a little deeper into this idea in chapter 4).

One who is called, for example into military service, also will receive specific training, clear instructions, and permanent guidance for his or her position of duty. This is what happens to every Christian in his or her particular area of ministry. God prepares those He calls and every believer is *called* to particular service in the body of Christ. God is not looking for a "few good men," as the Marines say. He is looking for every puzzle piece to fit correctly in its proper space. He is seeking to appoint runners to run with purpose.

## From Micro to Macro

This calling or appointment will span from specific to general, or from micro to macro. The 72 disciples in Luke 10 are receiving precise (micro) instructions as to where and how to go.

Now, though, let's discuss the macro appointment. We must answer the larger question, *"Why do I exist?"* In other words, what is our reason for being? It's a question most everyone asks at some point. *What is life all about?* Sadly, some spend their entire lives trying to figure out the answer.

I have asked many Christians the question, *"Why were you created?"* The answers vary, but usually go something like this, "We are created for worship." "I was created to love God." "To evangelize." "To serve others." While all of these answers are correct, former Princeton University President Jonathan Edwards noted that these are secondary goals falling under the one overriding goal: the glory of God. Edwards believed and logically supported the idea that God does everything for His glory, and this is the ultimate and central reality upon which all other truths hinge.

Generally speaking, a person will seek a secondary goal only in efforts to obtain something else more important. The secondary goal is only desired as a means of aiming at some further goal.

For example, suppose a man is afflicted with a disease and goes on a *journey* to find medicine. Obtaining the medicine is merely his secondary goal. He doesn't want to find medicine for medicine's sake, but rather as a means to a chief goal, which is healing and restored health. If the medicine doesn't help achieve his chief goal of restored health, then it's worthless and undesired. Thus, the medicine is merely a secondary goal. [11]

The *New England Primer* published in the 17th century asked the ancient questions of, "what and why," then answered in one short question, "What is the chief end of man?" The textbook concluded: Man's chief end is to glorify God and to enjoy Him forever. The 24 elders completely agree, falling on their faces to worship God forever, declaring, "You art

---

[11] Edwards, Jonathan. *The End for Which God Created the World: Updated to Modern English* (pp. 15-16). Glory Focus.

---

worthy, O Lord, to receive glory and honor and power: for You have created all things, and for Your pleasure, they are and were created."[12]

Thus, we were created, we exist, for the glory of God.

Don't miss this point: All that God does, He does for His glory, including our creation and call.

There is a reason a puzzle piece must be placed in its specific place, and the runner runs with an explicit message: for the glory of God. The prophet Isaiah writes that the Lord said, "I will say to the north, 'Give them up!' and to the south, 'Do not hold them back.' Bring my sons from afar and my daughters from the ends of the earth — everyone who is called by my name, *whom I created for my glory,* whom I formed and made" (Isaiah 43:6-7). And the apostle Paul agrees in 1 Corinthians 10:31: "So whether you eat or drink or whatever you do, *do it all for the glory of God.*"

**Big Question: What Is the Glory of God?**

Surprisingly, while many agree that we are created for the glory of God, most people cannot explain what that means. People sometimes say, "Give God the glory" or "To God be the glory." But can a person give God something, anything, to make Him greater than He already is? Obviously not. Isaiah says that our works and deeds are nothing more than filthy rags (Isaiah 64:6). The apostle Paul bluntly writes: "What is more, I consider everything a loss because of the surpassing worth of knowing Christ Jesus my Lord, for whose sake I have lost all things. I consider them garbage that I may gain Christ" (Philippians 3:8).

---

[12] Tozer, A. W. *The Pursuit of God* (pp. 289-291). Kindle Edition.

—

Several Bible translations use the word *rubbish* in place of garbage. *The Message* translation uses *dog dung*. The Greek term Paul uses is *skubala*, which is a vigorous and colorful word to grab the reader's attention, similar to the English term *poop*. In essence, Paul is saying, "The best this world can offer is like poop compared to the treasure of knowing Christ."

The world has nothing that can give God glory — only *we* can offer Him that by giving our lives completely and entirely to Him.

Many claim that Jesus will bring health, wealth, and a good life now. I have seen and given testimony to such blessings, but I also understand that any who seek Him primarily to serve their own interests will not find their soul's deepest satisfaction. "We are most satisfied with lives that bring God the greatest glory. None made in the image of God can find true fulfillment in paths that deny priority to God's glory."[13]

**Understand This!**

Above all, understand this: the phrase, "Give God glory" just means to pull back the veil, allowing God to be seen for who He is. The glory of God is the revelation of who He truly is.

The best part, as the apostle Paul explains, is that God has chosen us — His disciples — to make known His glory, for it is "Christ in you, the hope of glory" (Colossians 1:27). Did you catch that? The glory of God is the revelation of who He is, and He hopes to reveal himself through us as we *journey* together. As a matter of fact, there are people within our social networks who never will see God for who He is, if they

---

[13] Morgan, Christopher. *The Glory of God (Theology in Community)* (Kindle Location 4206). Crossway.

.

don't see Him in us.

This is key to a successful life *journey*: How can the world hear, see, observe, and contemplate "the glory of God" unless we, God's messengers, are sent? Amazing facilities, cutting-edge technology, and the latest and greatest evangelical programs can't give God glory for they are inanimate objects. "They may glorify God when done in faith. But it is always the Christ follower who will reveal His glory."[14]

Many of us are willing to be God-centered as long as we feel that God is man-centered. It is a subtle danger. We may think we are centering our lives on God, when we actually are making Him a means to self-esteem. Against this danger, "I urge you to ponder the implications of God loving His glory more than He loves us, and that this is the foundation of His love."[15]

The words of Christ in John 12:24-25 are self-explanatory: "Very truly I tell you, unless a kernel of wheat falls to the ground and dies, it remains only a single seed. But if it dies, it produces many seeds. Anyone who loves their life will lose it, while anyone who hates their life in this world will keep it for eternal life."

## The WOW Factor

I slipped into the back row of an Assembly of God church in Louisville, Kentucky. I was 17 and NOT chasing God, but a

---

[14] Luther, Martin (2012-05-17). *Concerning Christian Liberty* (p. 23). Kindle Edition.
[15] Piper, John (2013-01-31). *Brothers, We Are Not Professionals: A Plea to Pastors for Radical Ministry*, updated and expanded edition (pp. 187-190). Kindle Edition.

girl! That is when the gospel impacted my life through Pastor W.L. Rodgers; God used Rodgers to astonish me, what I like to call the WOW Factor. "It didn't happen overtly, or through brutal intimidation, but rather via an organic and persuasive revelation of God's glory that compelled me to follow Jesus."[16]

The glory of God is that WOW Factor. And the crazy thing is that God wants to WOW the world through us.[17] Christ in you, the hope of *WOW!* Today, men and women who are following Jesus at all costs WOW me. My wife falls into this category, as do my children and grandchildren. It is Jesus in them that keeps bringing me back to His glory, His revelation, His image.

## Ichabod

In 1989, when Connie and I arrived in Cuenca, Ecuador — a city of 250,000 inhabitants and less than 1,000 baptized evangelical Christians — I was determined to build the largest evangelical church Cuenca had ever seen. We accomplished this, but not without paying a price.

Construction was difficult and expensive. The sacrifices were great, and one of our young men died during the building of the church. By building a megachurch with great programs, facilities, and systems, we marched in lockstep with other "successful" ministries of the day.

We had agendas, programs, causes, activities, and ministries.

---

[16] Greenleaf, Robert (2012-07-10). *The Servant as Leader* (p. 582). The Greenleaf Center for Servant Leadership.
[17] 1 Corinthians 1:27.

However, I must confess that at times we didn't have the right purpose. We had a *good* purpose, but not the *right* purpose.

If you would have asked members of our congregation about our goal, most probably would have responded about what our church was doing as a congregation to impact a city.

I would be remiss if I didn't note that the church we built, physically and spiritually, has indeed served the city well and has drawn many into a relationship with Jesus. But I can't help but wonder if I only determined to build a great *temple* in order that *I might* WOW the city. Great temples, cathedrals, and statues constructed in the name of Jesus have impressed people for centuries. In modern times, shows and music and lights and sound WOW churchgoers. But are we bringing glory to God through these advancements? I am not saying that massive programs and technological wonders are a distraction, but we must be careful not to believe they bring glory to God, either. Again, these devices and tools may be used to the glory of God when done in faith, but it is always the follower of Christ who will reveal His glory.[18]

If we build our programs and edifices to impress a city and draw a crowd, our efforts will leave us as empty as any social program the world has to offer. And it will leave pastors, leaders, and laypeople feeling empty and dead. It is not the empty church building that concerns me; it is the empty congregants gathering in impressive structures and engaging in programs. It's not a stretch to think the word *Ichabod*[19] — "Where is the Glory?" — could describe some of our greatest "Christian" achievements.

---

[18] Luther, Martin (2012-05-17*). Concerning Christian Liberty* (p. 15). Kindle Edition.
[19] 1 Samuel 4:19-22.

## Jesus' Thoughts from the Cross

What was on Jesus' mind during His crucifixion? Did He think about all the great cathedrals that would be built in His name? Did He reflect on the great worldwide institutions that would carry His name or the armies that would march under the symbol of the Cross on which He hung? Or maybe the millions of dollars that would be spent on jewelry shaped to resemble His instrument of execution? Amazingly, but unsurprisingly, Jesus thought of the one dying beside Him. Jesus thought about bringing glory to the Father by revealing God to a fellow Jew condemned for breaking the laws of the land.

If we are ever going to impact our communities, we must acknowledge, accept, and apply the first of these 13 words: appointed. If we lose touch with our chosen-ness, we expose ourselves to the temptation of self-rejection, and that temptation undermines the possibility of ever growing as disciples. As we grow as His disciples with an assignment and appointment to bring glory to God, it will not be the verbal exchange of information that is the most potent witness to unbelievers. The most powerful witness will be the community of believers living in the presence, power, and purpose of Christ."[20]

The success of our *journey* rests upon this first word in our study: Appointed. When God's creatures know His excellent qualities, love Him for possessing these qualities, and rejoice in Him, we are properly exercising and expressing honor and praise to Him. But all of this can be summarized under one phrase — the glory of God — which is the revelation of who

---

[20] Nouwen, Henri J. M. *Life of the Beloved: Spiritual Living in a Secular World* (p. 56). The Crossroad Publishing Company.

---

He really is. We must understand this point well.[21]

Now that we know why we exist, our <u>appointment</u>, we have another question to answer: With whom will I go on this *journey?*

---

[21] Edwards, Jonathan (2014-12-13). *The End for Which God Created the World: Updated to Modern English* (p. 186). Glory Focus.

# S.T.O.P.

**Consider again the key word <u>Appointed</u>, and ask yourself the following questions:**

What was Jesus conveying to His disciples through the use of the word <u>Appointed</u>?


What did Jesus want them to understand by using this term?


What does the word <u>Appointed</u> now mean to me?


What does Jesus want to convey to me through this word?


**Now let's live it out. How will you respond to what you have heard, read, learned, or felt inspired to do?**

S. SPECIFIC: What specifically will you do in response to the key word <u>Appointed</u>?


T. TIME-SENSITIVE: Within what time frame will you begin or complete the task?


O. OBTAINABLE: Is it possible? If not, go back to S.


P. PERTINENT: How does this goal relate to the key word and our understanding of it?


*Read It - Think It - Write It - Share It*

---

# 2

## Word Two – Two
### *Community Caravan*

Key word: Two – The sum of one and one [22]

Key verse: "...sent them two by two ahead of Him to every town and place where He was about to go..." Luke 10:1

Key thought: The micro and macro calls are fulfilled through living in community. And that community should be on the move. It's a lot like a caravan of believers.

───────────

Understanding why we exist (chapter one) is key to implementing the other steps of the *journey*. The word *two* shows us that this fundamental reason for existence is to be lived out in a community as our underlying foundation.
A great Old Testament example of this is found in the story of Ruth.[23]

> Then they lifted up their voices and wept again. And Orpah kissed her mother-in-law, but Ruth clung to her. And she said, 'See, your sister-in-law has gone back to her people and to her gods; return after your sister-in-law.' But Ruth said, 'Do not urge me to leave

───────────────

[22] Oxford Dictionaries.
[23] For a modern version of this biblical story, I recommend *Annabelle's Ruth* by Betty Thomason Owens.

you or to return from following you. For where you go I will go, and where you lodge, I will lodge. Your people shall be my people, and your God my God. Where you die I will die, and there will I be buried. May the Lord do so to me and more also if anything but death parts me from you.' And when Naomi saw that she was determined to go with her, she said no more.

Ruth 1:14-18 is a reaffirmation of the wise man's phrase, "Two are better than one." [24]

## Two Are Better Than One

Connie and our daughter, Leah, dropped off Joil, Leah's husband, and me on the western slopes of the Andes Mountains, 1,000 feet below the Continental Divide. In 36 hours, they'd pick us up on the eastern slopes, some 4,000 feet below the divide. The hike would include an overnight stay and 18 hours of hiking on the old Inca trail that originally ran from the Pacific Coast to the heart of the Inca Empire in Cuenca, Ecuador.

Chachis (runners) used to carry fresh fish over this very trail from the ocean to the Inca in Cuenca on a daily basis.
Joil and I would not be doing any running with fish in our hands or baskets, but we would follow the sometimes-perilous trail for the next day and a half.
As we did, we ascended to 14,000 feet, marveled at the view from the Continental Divide, then made our way to Osohuyco Lake, where we would fish and camp for the night.

---

[24] Ecclesiastes 4: 9–10.

That was the plan, anyway. Those who have traveled, vacationed, or worked with me know that my adventures usually involve a risk bordering on stupidity. Kirk Noonan, a friend who has assisted me in writing, can attest. Kirk will never forget the night we drove shrouded in darkness and dense fog from the capital of Ecuador to the Pacific coast. The roads had no guardrails, lighting, or asphalt. The fog prevented us from seeing sheer drops of thousands of feet.

The hike with Joil proved to be a similar adventure, carrying risks of its own. As we fished for trout on the banks of the lake, I slipped and slid right into the frigid waters. Immediately I struggled to pull myself from the lake and called out to Joil for help as hyperthermia set in.

I quickly removed my clothing and slipped into my sleeping bag that Joil had pulled from my pack. He then set up our tent and built a fire. Needless to say, I survived. But if Joil hadn't been with me, I probably would have died. Two are better than one. Experiencing life with others is not only exhilarating, but also necessary for success. "Two are better than one because they have a good return for their labor: If either of them falls, one can help the other up. But pity anyone who falls (into a lake!) and has no one to help them up" (Ecclesiastes 4: 9–10).

Both of my community stories are enveloped in a *journey*. That's why I have titled this chapter Community Caravan. We are in a community that is — or should be — on the move.

**Community Allows Shared Inspiration**

Community gives one the opportunity to *journey* with a host of dissimilar travelers. That is the absolute beauty of community. Our weirdness, faults, warts, egos, talents, and lost-ness paint a fantastic puzzle scene, with each piece filling what would be an obvious hole in the Master's design. Some of my greatest inspirations have come from Christian brothers and sisters whom I have lovingly nicknamed Davy Crockett, Dora, and Beetlejuice. (Yep, every congregation has one. And sometimes I am that one.) But it is the strange beside the familiar, the peculiar with the ordinary, and the colorful near the bland, that makes a beautiful collage we call community. Anything less would be lifeless playacting.

> "And let us consider how we may spur one another on toward love and good deeds, not giving up meeting together, as some are in the habit of doing, but encouraging one another — and all the more as you see the Day approaching" (Hebrews 10:24-25).

## Community Brings Joy and Happiness

"Son, get out of bed, you will be late for church," a mother exhorts. "But mom, I don't want to; it's so boring."

Then the mother sighs, "But son, you must. You're the pastor."

Oh, we can be a boring group of congregants. But community, on the other hand, is entirely different. It's a time to catch up, share a burden, shed a tear, embrace a friend. "How good and pleasant it is when God's people live together in unity!" (Psalm 133:1).

## Community Fosters Confrontations

I know what you are thinking: "What? Confrontation?" But as we are painfully aware, true family and community — especially when traveling together — requires some confrontation along the way. We cannot get through life without conflict, even if only with ourselves. This is the rub that polishes the roughest of stones.

> "Bear with each other and forgive one another if any of you has a grievance against someone. Forgive as the Lord forgave you. And over all these virtues put on love, which binds them all together in perfect unity" (Colossians 3:13–14).

## Community Nurtures Spiritual Empowerment

"When two or three are gathered in my name I will be in the midst of them" (Matthew 18:20a). But isn't He always with us? After all, His name is Emmanuel, God with us. And Jesus promised, "I will be with you always, even to the end of the age" (Matthew 28:20b). Yes, He is always present, but when we gather as a community of faith, His presence is physical through the presence of other believers. An excellent example of this was the first century church, which made a habit of meeting together, eating together, and worshipping together. As a result, "the Lord added to their number daily those who were being saved" (Acts 2:46–47).

Being in church on Sundays is important. But if you want to be a Christ follower, you must be one every day in the context of all your community of faith connections. That's where you'll see ministry happen.[25]

---

[25] Stewardship Team, February 3, 2017, "*4 Reasons the Bible Calls Us to Community*" Stewardship.com *www.stewardship.com/articles/4-reasons-the-bible-calls-us-to-community.*

---

## Community Is Life-Giving

It can be hard for some of us to commit to community, especially if we're guarded or prefer solitude. But community is God's desire for us — and a sign of a mature faith. Ultimately, when we grow in our relationships with others, we're growing in relationship with Him.[26]

Paul's teaching on spiritual transformation in Romans 12 and in his epistles always happens in the context of community — the body of Christ with its many members. We are given to one another in the body of Christ for mutual edification and to spur one another on to love and good deeds. Gifts are not bestowed on us for our own benefit or self-aggrandizement, but rather that we can be agents of grace for one another, building up the body, of which we are only one part.

As author Robert Mulholland writes, "We can no more be conformed to the image of Christ outside corporate spirituality than a coal can continue to burn outside of the fire."

While our spiritual practices certainly include private disciplines (solitude and silence, prayer and meditation, Scripture reading, self-examination and confession, retreat, spiritual direction), to be effective they also must include disciplines in community (corporate prayer and worship, teaching, Communion, Sabbath, hospitality, caring for those in need, spiritual friendship and direction), and engagement with the world (evangelism, caring for the poor, compassion, justice, etc.).[27]

---

[26] Ibid.
[27] Barton, Ruth Haley. *Pursuing God's Will Together: A Discernment Practice for Leadership Groups* (The Transforming Center Set) (pp. 244-245). InterVarsity.

---

## Community Promotes Contagious Behavior

Jesus instructed His disciples to go <u>two</u> by <u>two</u>. Forming a community to live out the discipleship *journey* is essential, for it is the breeding ground for contagious behavior. We know too well that our styles, fads, addictions, and activities are driven mostly by those with whom we associate and live. Good or bad, our family, friends and social networks mold us.

I like to invite my disciples to apply this simple test by asking themselves, "Are my present relationships pulling me up, or am I pulling up others in my community?" If the answer to both is no, you might want to question the process you are using to allow influencers into your life or communities.

## Community Builds a Solid Team

Many times I have seen ministries and businesses trying to employ the term *team,* thinking that the use of the word will somehow make a difference.

However, if you do not understand how your coworker's efforts should intersect with your efforts, how can you truly be a team? If you don't understand how your actions and reactions directly affect someone else's actions and reactions, you are reduced to a group of individual teams playing on one field, running your plays in separate games.

In his book, *The Five Dysfunctions of a Team*, Patrick Lencioni writes, "If you could get all the people in an organization rowing in the same direction, you could dominate any industry, in any market, against any competition, at any time."[28]

---

[28] Lencioni, Patrick M. (2011-11-17). *The Five Dysfunctions of a Team, Enhanced Edition: A Leadership Fable* (J-B Lencioni Series) (p. 2). Wiley.

---

Our friends Mark and Dee Lehmann pastor Cornerstone Church, a vibrant and growing congregation in Bowie, Maryland. Their staff is a team, but no one doubts who the quarterback is. Mark spends a significant portion of his time hearing from God and discerning God's will for the church. Then, in their "skull sessions," his staff members work through the plays as a team. Team means that everyone knows the exact movements of the other players, and each is responsible for executing his or her particular pattern. When they win a down, they win as a team, but when they lose a down, the quarterback accepts the challenge and responsibility to make a better call.

## Community Breeds Discipleship

After hearing for years some disturbing statistics concerning ministry burnout, I pleasantly read Barna Group's new report that pastors report higher levels of satisfaction than U.S. adults overall. [29]

Barna did note that 35 percent of pastors are frustrated with the lack of commitment among laypeople and 27 percent are concerned with the low level of spiritual maturity among churchgoers. Both of these issues can be traced back to the lack of true biblical community. We should reflect on Dietrich Bonhoeffer's warning, "The person who loves their dream of community will destroy community [even if their intentions are ever so earnest], but the individual who loves those around them will create community." [30]

---

[29] 2017 Barna Group. (2017-02-15). *www.barna.com/research/healthy-pastors-relationships/*Research Releases in Leaders & Pastors.
[30] Bonhoeffer, Dietrich (2012-06-19). *Life Together* (pp. 109-110). Hymns Ancient and Modern Ltd.

.

## Community Combats Individualism

Let's be honest. We cannot equate sitting in church with community. Just because we are members does not mean we are a team. Simply being in the same building at the same time doesn't make our positive behaviors contagious. We must be diligent, purposeful, and deliberate to become community. Sadly, we have moved in the opposite direction in recent years. That might be a contributing factor in the growth of the megachurch. For some, a large congregation is a place to fulfill a social, religious obligation without entering true community. Fortunately, most of these grand churches are continuously looking for new ways to bring small groups and community to their congregants.

I recently read the following social media Christian advertisement: "The most important thing you can teach the kids in your life is to have a personal relationship with the Lord."

Maybe it should read, "The most important thing you can teach the kids in your life is to have a *communal* relationship with the Lord." For the gospel is not a purely personal matter. It has a social dimension. It is a communal affair. To embrace the gospel, then, is to enter into community. A person cannot have one without the other.[31]

Frank Viola and George Barna suggest that the primary goal of the Church has shifted from experiencing and expressing the Lord Jesus Christ corporately to the making of individual converts.

---

[31] Banks, Robert J. (1994-02-01). *Paul's Idea of Community: The Early House Churches in Their Cultural Setting,* Revised edition (pp. 639-642). Baker Book Group.

---

Though the Church rightly believes Christ's atonement is absolutely essential to getting humanity back on track, God's eternal purpose includes enlarging the eternal fellowship He has with His Son and making it visible on planet Earth — the glory of God![32]

We are not called to build preaching stations, or view performances by pulpit personalities as the dominating attraction for church. These could be secondary goals, but we are called to live out our faith in a *real and living community* that reflects the glory of God. Evangelist John Wesley understood the dangers of the tendency to live out one's faith independent of a community of believers. He wrote, "Christianity is essentially a social religion ... to turn it into a 'solitary' religion is indeed to destroy it."[33]

Yet we seem to continue down this path of individualism over community. And why? Maybe it's just the way we have always done it and doing anything else just doesn't feel right. Hopefully we have not fallen into the error of pragmatism. Again, in their book, *Pagan Christianity?: Exploring the Roots of Our Church Practices,* Viola and Barna write:

> "Pragmatism is unspiritual, not just because it encourages ethical considerations to be secondary, but because it depends on techniques rather than on God to produce the desired effects ...Pragmatism is harmful because it teaches "the end justifies the means."

> If the end is considered "holy," just about any "means" are acceptable. The philosophy of pragmatism

---

[32]Viola, Frank and Barna, George. *Pagan Christianity?: Exploring the Roots of Our Church Practices*, Tyndale Momentum.

[33] Deck, Ray, III. (2013-09-30).
https://blog.faithlife.com/blog/2013/09/the-4-rules-of-communication/.

---

opens the door for human manipulation and a complete reliance upon oneself rather than upon God."[34]

## Community Is Essential for Checks and Balances

Have you ever gone fishing and prayed to catch just one? Then upon catching the fish, you quickly prayed, "Lord, just one more." The "just one more" never satisfies us. It's the "next one" that we think will bring the greatest satisfaction. "More, more, more" is Satan's favorite line to destroy followers of Christ. Jesus made it clear that this way of thinking leaves one empty. "If you cling to your life, you will lose it; but if you give up your life for Me, you will find it" (Matthew 10:39, NLT).

I equate that mentality to winning. Ever notice how winning gives us a feeling of power? This is true in sports, politics, and even in the church. Many of us want to win no matter the cost.

Truth be told, in my carnality, I want to be better than everyone else. True community, however, will keep our desire for winning in check. When we begin to live for the benefit of others, we will truly win, for their success becomes our own success. I can't help but wonder what would happen if we began to see other people's victories as our own. If we are going to fulfill the Great Commission by going and making disciples, we must do so in community.

And that's best done with a humble stance: Word 3 will bring us to just that.

---

[34] Frank Viola; George Barna. *Pagan Christianity?: Exploring the Roots of Our Church Practices* (Kindle Location 837). Kindle Edition.

---

# S.T.O.P.

**Consider the word <u>Two</u> again and ask yourself the following:**

What was Jesus teaching His disciples through the use of the word <u>Two</u>?

What did Jesus want them to comprehend?

What does this word now mean to me?

What does Jesus want to teach me through this word?

**Now let's live it out. How will you respond to what you have heard, read, learned, or felt inspired to do?**

S. SPECIFIC: What exactly will you do in response to this word?

T. TIME-SENSITIVE: Within what time frame will you begin or complete the task?

O. OBTAINABLE: Is it possible? If not, go back to S.

P. PERTINENT: How does this goal relate to the key word and your understanding of it?

*Read It - Think It - Write It - Share It*

# 3

## Word Three – Ask
### *Poignant Petition*

Key word: Ask – To call for; need; require. [35]

Key verse: "Ask the Lord of the harvest, therefore, to send out workers into His harvest field" (Luke 10:2).

Key thought: Words 1 and 2, Appointed and Two, call for mental, spiritual and emotional preparations for the *Journey*. Word 3, however, is a call to action; it's a call to ask.

---

An unnamed reporter labeled Pastor Charles Spurgeon "redolent of bad taste, vulgar, and theatrical."[36] But no observers ever doubted his sincerity. And when he called men and women to pray, he made his appeal with all the theatrics within him:

> Sons of God cannot live without prayer. They are wrestling Jacobs. They are men in whom the Holy Ghost so works, that they can no more live without prayer than I can live without breathing. They must pray. Sirs, mark you, if you are living without prayer,

---

[35] Oxford Dictionaries
[36] Spurgeon, Charles. *The Complete Works of Charles Spurgeon: Volume 1, Sermons 1-53* (pp. 602-606). Delmarva Publications.

you are living without Christ; and dying like that, your portion will be in the lake which burneth with fire. God redeem you, God rescue you from such a lot! But you who are "the sons of Jacob," take comfort, for God is immutable.[37]

Jesus' call to prayer in Luke 10 is not nearly as dramatic; it is, however, the first item on His to-do list. Somehow, however, I failed to understand the necessity for His disciples to <u>ask</u> Jesus to send workers into His service. From my first concepts of God, faith, and church, I have understood the importance of prayer. I can remember going to novena[38] prayer services in the Catholic church with my mom on Wednesday nights. I retreated with my father at Gethsemane Monastery in Bardstown, Kentucky, where silence and prayer are the pledges of the movement. Yet, even as an adult believer, I could not fully understand why Jesus calls on His disciples to <u>ask</u> for laborers. Does God really need me to <u>ask</u> Him to send workers? Doesn't He already desire to do so?

An interesting story from Mark's gospel introduces us to blind Bartimaeus and sheds light on the power of <u>asking</u>:

"Then they came to Jericho. As Jesus and his disciples, together with a large crowd, were leaving the city, a blind man, Bartimaeus, was sitting by the roadside begging. When he heard that it was Jesus of Nazareth, he began to shout, 'Jesus, Son of David, have mercy on me!' Many rebuked him and told him

---

[37] Ibid.
[38] The word NOVENA is taken from "novem," the Latin word for nine. A NOVENA is made up of nine days of PRAYER and meditation usually to ask God for special PRAYER requests or petitions.

to be quiet, but he shouted all the more, 'Son of David, have mercy on me!' Jesus stopped and said, 'Call him.' So they called to the blind man, 'Cheer up! On your feet! He's calling you.' Throwing his cloak aside, he jumped to his feet and came to Jesus. 'What do you want Me to do for you?' Jesus <u>asked</u> him. The blind man said, 'Rabbi, I want to see.' 'Go,' said Jesus, 'your faith has healed you.' Immediately he received his sight and followed Jesus along the road" (Mark 10:46-52).

Obviously, Bartimaeus is blind. Jesus undoubtedly knows this, yet He <u>asks</u> Bartimaeus, "What do you want Me to do for you?" "Rabbi, I want to see," he replied. Seemingly, Jesus needs Bartimaeus to <u>ask</u>. But why? Does <u>asking</u> change God? From my experience, I have learned that <u>asking</u> changes *everything* because <u>asking</u> changes us! It changes our circumstances, our perspective, our desires, our wants, and our needs. <u>Asking</u> God to intervene in our situation changes everything.

To <u>ask</u> is defined as, "to request for a need or desire." I've always understood it to mean that I should call upon God to send someone, a laborer, to places of need. <u>Asking</u> in the context of Luke 10, however, is to <u>ask</u> for someone to go in *my* place. See the difference?

It brings to mind a common practice from the U.S. Civil War: the procurement of a mercenary combatant. For as little as $300, an individual could hire a soldier to serve in his place.

We need missionaries to serve on our behalf throughout the world in harvest fields that we can never reach, while we are tending to the harvest field where God has placed us.

This is quite sobering. Can you imagine hiring a surrogate

warrior to fight and to suffer, or even to die in one's place? But when we pray to the Lord of the Harvest to send forth laborers, that is exactly what we are doing. We pray that He will send laborers because we can't go, or maybe because we just won't go.

Today, your harvest field may simply be your neighborhood, workplace, community, or even your grocery store. But even while you're tending your fields, pray for God to send others to the remote, undesirable depots the gospel has not yet reached.

## We're Invited and Commanded to <u>Ask</u>. Are We <u>Asking</u>?

Jesus' call to <u>ask</u> is genuine, and the command is mutually beneficial. Reliance on God leads us to <u>ask</u> what He needs from us, and what we need from Him. The Scriptures clearly and continually point to the fact God is always in control. And when we understand and apply this truth, we will encourage faith and temper anxiety.

"We are not to presume on God's automatic care, but rather to come in trusting dependence to <u>ask</u> for what we need," says Mary Anne Voelkel, veteran missionary and former prayer coordinator for InterVarsity Christian Fellowship.

Jesus makes it clear when He says in Matthew 7:7-11, "<u>Ask</u>, and it will be given to you; seek and you will find; knock and the door will be opened to you. For everyone who <u>asks</u> receives; the one who seeks finds; and to the one who knocks, the door will be opened. If you, then, though you are evil, know how to give good gifts to your children, how much more will your Father in heaven give good gifts to those who <u>ask</u> Him."

---

"Since God is a Spirit and we cannot see Him, perhaps our interactive prayer communication encourages our faith and develops intimacy and dependence," Voelkel continues. "In our materialistic world, it is so easy to let God provide everything we need and then assume that it 'just happened' or that we did it ourselves. In asking, we acknowledge our dependence."[39]

## Asking Will Align Us with God's Will.
## Are We Asking?

Knowing the next step of God's plan will depend upon our communication with the plan giver. Our prayer of asking is faith personified; we put breath, flesh, and voice to our confidence that it is God who works in us to will and to act in order to fulfill His good purpose.[40]

We discover this truth in Mark's report of what happened after a hectic day of teaching and healing: "Very early in the morning, while it was still dark, Jesus got up, left the house and went off to a solitary place, where He prayed" (Mark 1:35).

Jesus prayerfully waited for his Father's instructions. Jesus had no divinely drawn blueprint or schedule; He discerned the Father's will day by day in a life of prayer. Because of this, He resisted the urgent demands of others and focused on the important functions of His mission.[41]

---

[39] Voelkel, Mary Anne. (2016-08-12) "If God Is In Control, Why Do We Pray?" https://studentsoul.intervarsity.org/why-pray, Student Soul, Intervarsity.
[40] Philippians 2:12-13.
[41] Hummel, Charles E. Tyranny of the Urgent (pp. 80-84). InterVarsity Press.

Living in alignment with God's will is not about aligning God with our plan or changing His will to fit ours, but rather about us coming into an alliance with God's heart.

The following devotional thought by an unknown author explains, "I no longer pray to try to change God's mind, to influence or persuade God to do what I want to be done. I name and lift my problems and concerns to God (and try to let them go, too) and I ask God's deep presence in each of these situations — problems, people, and so on. Then, I try to trust."

## Asking Empowers Us.
## Are We Asking?

"When we pray, Satan trembles," John Bisagno writes in *The Power of Positive Praying.* "When we pray, heaven's gates open wide. When we pray, desperation fades, and trials wither before us like grass before the scorching sun. When we pray, power comes, love fills our heart, and life is filled with song."[42] Poets will get this truth straight when the rest of us struggle to grasp it.

Consider the words of Reuben Morgan in the popular Hillsong United song "You Said":

> *You said, "Ask and you will*
> *receive whatever you need."*
> *You said, "Pray and I'll hear from*
> *heaven and I'll heal your land."*
> *You said, "Your glory will fill the*
> *earth like water, the sea."*
> *You said, "Lift up your eyes, the*
> *harvest is here, yes the Kingdom is near."*

---

[42] Bisagno, John R. *The Power of Positive Praying,* (p. 15), B&H Books.

*You said, "Ask and I'll give the nations to you."*
*Oh, Lord, that's the cry of my heart.*
*Distant shores and the islands will see*
*Your light, as it rises on us.*

Let's not merely pray for a better place in line or for God to bless the hands that prepared the food. Let's pray powerful prayers that God's Kingdom would come to our communities and that His will would be done throughout the nations of the world.

## Asking Humbles Us.
## Are We Asking?

In some respects, asking in prayer puts us in an extreme position of vulnerability. Think about it. When we ask for something, we expose our needs and weaknesses. When we ask, we humbly confess, "I can't do this alone" or "I need help" or "I want something You have."

As I mentioned earlier, it's interesting that Jesus implores God to send workers into His harvest field as a first step in going. Perhaps Jesus is teaching His disciples valuable lessons about humility and their neediness. Maybe He's inviting them to a level of dependency on Him like He is modeling dependence on God so that something greater — something even supernatural — can happen. In John 16:23, Jesus tells His disciples, "Very truly I tell you, my Father will give you whatever you ask in My name."

What does that mean, and how does it connect with going? I believe the answer can be found in God's yearning to communicate, collaborate, and cooperate with us in carrying out His desire to see everyone turn from sin and commit his or her life to Jesus.

—

Yes, the act of <u>asking</u> humbles us. It shouts *We need help!* It places us squarely in a position of dependency, but it also sets the stage for God to do the miraculous. Jesus knows His disciples are eager to go. He knows their intentions are great. The Lord sees that they're willing to go to the ends of the earth for Him. Instead of blindly green-lighting the adventure, He commands them to <u>ask</u> God to send them out, just before imploring them to go.

Jesus knows what they'll face. He realizes the days ahead won't be easy. He understands what they're going to need. He expects overdoses of boldness, fearlessness, and strength are in order. In other words, He's telling them they're going to need supernatural intervention.

## <u>Asking</u> Is Communication.
## Are We <u>Asking</u>?

When we <u>ask</u> God for anything, we are communicating with the Creator of the Universe. By <u>asking</u>, we are acknowledging our dependence on Him. That's quite an honor. No matter who we are, how much money we make, or what neighborhood we're from, we can have an audience with the Creator of the Universe and can <u>ask</u> for anything.

When you start <u>asking</u>, you'll be surprised how your life begins to sparkle with the presence of God.[43] Don't we enjoy and cherish the opportunities to spend time with those who are concerned for our well-being? The prayers of Jesus for His disciples in John 17 and Luke 22 show the intensity of His prayers as He prays with and for friends. It was not a to-do list, wish list, or grocery list. His prayers are profound and heartfelt communion born out of concern, pain, and anguish.

---

[43] Miller, Paul. *A Praying Life: Connecting with God in a Distracting World* (p. 150). NavPress.

Eugenia Brown, a history instructor at Edgewood College, agrees. She sees prayer not so much as a list of wants or a way to change God's mind, but rather as a process to regain perspective in one's relationship with God. As with Jesus, she says, "We pray to deepen our relationship with God. We pray to remind ourselves of our place of humility, to remind ourselves that God is God, and we are not. To submit myself to God in prayer changes me. I believe that God loves me enough to want to transform me into all that God created me to be, but I must cooperate in that transformation. Every time I pray, I cooperate just a little bit more."[44]

Be sure that when one begins to ask, God will respond. And when we ask or intercede for others, as Jesus calls us to do in Luke 10, He will respond to others' needs as well. When we put this in the light of going, it reveals the heart of God — that none should perish.

The apostle Peter writes, "The Lord is not slow in keeping his promise, as some understand slowness. Instead, He is patient with you, not wanting anyone to perish, but everyone to come to repentance" (2 Peter 3:9).

Our needs today, as we *journey* missionally, are the same as the disciples of 2,000 years ago. We need to be on the side of the Creator of the Universe, protecting and providing for us as only He can. Without Him, our mission is a lost, impossible cause. But after all, aren't we called to take on invincible giants? It begins by asking.

---

[44] Brown, Eugenia, *If God Is in Control, Why Do We Pray?* Student Soul Intervarsity.

---

---

59

In our offices at Unsión in Cuenca, Ecuador, no one is permitted to say, "That's not my job." If we can't find an answer, we look for one. If it's not our job, we find whose job it is. And if nothing else, we just make it our job. Yet, the church is quite guilty of saying precisely that to the Harvest Master. The word *responsible* is made up of two parts, Response and Able, or "Able to Respond." We must be responsible disciples of Christ, having the ability to respond to the need for workers, and that response begins with asking.

> "The harvest is plentiful, but the workers are few. Ask the Lord of the harvest, therefore, to send out workers into his harvest field. Go! I am sending you out like lambs among wolves. Do not take a purse or bag or sandals; and do not greet anyone on the road" (Luke 10:2-4).

These words, recorded nearly two millennia ago, have never been more relevant than today. When Jesus spoke these words, fewer than 300 million people lived in the world. Today, 7.5 billion people live on the planet. And to win this enormous exploding population, we will need to ask.

We can point to church growth in some sectors of the world and exciting accomplishments in others, but the truth is that there are more people, at this very moment, living without Christ than ever in the history of the world. That's sobering and profoundly disturbing. Are we asking?

If you are like me, you are concerned that we have family, friends, colleagues, and neighbors who have yet to come to faith in Jesus Christ. If that does not concern me, I might just be placating to Christianity. But if we are sincere about the *journey* of faith, we must begin to ask.

---

60

God is in the business of turning the tide. We need to <u>ask</u> God to send us — or someone in our place — into our mission fields boldly, with the confidence that He will provide the right words, ideas, strength, fortitude, and opportunities to share the love of Christ. We have to collaborate with the Creator of the Universe if we want to see those we love and care for make the only decision — accepting Christ as their Savior — that matters eternally. But this begins with His disciples <u>asking</u>.

It is imperative at the outset that we come to terms with this simple, yet life-changing truth: God is for you. If you don't believe that, then you'll pray small, timid prayers; if you are convinced it's true, then you'll pray faith-filled, audacious prayers. And one way or another, your small, timid prayers or faith-filled audacious prayers will change the trajectory of your life. The path you choose will determine what kind of person you will be.

Pastor and author Mark Batterson teaches that prayers are prophecies. They are the best predictors of your spiritual future. Who you become is determined by how you pray. Ultimately, the transcript of your petitions before God become the script of your life.[45] For as we delight in the Lord, He will give us the desires of our heart (Psalms 37:4). Let's begin to <u>ask</u> big!

Charles Sheldon's famous question, "What would Jesus do?" is an excellent way to measure our discipleship *journey*. After we have <u>asked</u> the Holy Spirit to tell us what Jesus would do and have received an answer, we are to act in obedience regardless of the outcome.

---

[45] Batterson, Mark. *The Circle Maker: Praying Circles Around Your Biggest Dreams and Greatest Fears* (pp. 78-82). Zondervan.

If the goal is to act just as He did, then we have no option but to <u>ask</u>, powerfully and continually, that He, the Lord of the Harvest, would send forth laborers in our place.[46] Could we, would we be brave enough to pray the prayer of Isaiah, "Lord, here I am, send me!"

**It's Okay to Keep <u>Asking</u>**

As we come into powerful communion and alignment with the Father through prayers of <u>asking</u>, we can be confident that we can keep <u>asking</u> on behalf of others, and even ourselves. We are commanded to do so.

"Yet you have not called on me, Jacob, you have not wearied yourselves for me, Israel" (Isaiah 43:22). And what if we are <u>asking</u> wrongly? Don't worry about <u>asking</u> in error. Continual communion with the Father will eventually work the bugs out of our erroneous prayers.

Our problem is not that we pray incorrectly; our problem is that we just quit <u>asking</u>. And here is the real answer: ask, <u>ask</u> again, <u>ask</u> one more time, then, ask again ... You get the picture.

Coming up: let's get going! Word Four is GO!

---

[46] Sheldon, Charles Monroe. *In His Steps* (p. 15). Kindle edition.

# S.T.O.P.

**Look at the key word <u>Ask</u> again and consider the following questions:**

What was Jesus conveying to His disciples through the word <u>Ask</u>?

What did Jesus want them to understand?

What does the word <u>Ask</u> now mean to me?

What does Jesus want to convey to me through this word?

**Now let's live it out. How will you respond to what you have heard, read, learned, or felt inspired to do?**

S. SPECIFIC: What specifically will you do in response to the word <u>Ask</u>?

T. TIME-SENSITIVE: Within what time frame will you begin or complete the task?

O. OBTAINABLE: Is it possible? If not, go back to S.

P. PERTINENT: How does this goal relate to the word <u>Ask</u> and our understanding of it?

*Read It - Think It - Write It - Share It*

# PART TWO
## *Step the step*

Key words four and five: Go – Wolves

As we noticed in part one of our study of Luke 10:1-9, the text will cause the reader to ask reflective questions: What is my mission or appointment? Who is with me, who is my team? Why is asking important to the process?

Sadly, many plans are made only to later be discarded due to any number of challenges, burdens, or distractions. For that reason, I believe Jesus leads His disciples to the first physical steps of this *journey*, go, among the wolves.

## STEPS

Steps go up. Steps go down.
They wind through woods. They march to town.

Steps made of marble, steps of stone
rise in rows or sit alone.

Steps worn with sadness, steps forsaken —
yet those most wasted are steps not taken.

—W.E.M.

*"In their hearts humans plan their course, but the Lord establishes their steps" (Proverbs 16:9).*

—

# 4

## Word Four - Go
### *Motivated Movement*

Key word: <u>Go</u> – To withdraw one's self, to go away, depart.[47]

Key verse: "<u>Go</u>!" (Luke 10:3)

Key thought: The word *journey* in itself conveys the idea of movement. As gears in a clock, some move quickly, others in reverse and a few nearly motionless, yet all are moving for the same purpose and in perfect harmony.

---

As with many hobbies, sailing has taught me a valuable life lesson or two. Among the most important lesson is that a sailboat cannot turn unless it's moving. The same is true of people. If they aren't moving, it's almost impossible to get them to turn. Maybe that's why Jesus tells His disciples, "<u>Go</u>!" In modern slang, His words are more blunt: "Get moving!" Jesus urges action because He knows that people, like boats, don't turn unless they are moving. Jesus did not say "One day you must go." He said, "<u>Go</u>!"

We need to live like verbs rather than nouns. Jesus wants us moving so we can fully take advantage of situations when the Holy Spirit creates moments of opportunity. For until he is moved by the Divine Spirit, no person can tell what he may

---

[47] Greek Lexicon. G5217 (KJV), *Blue Letter Bible*.

do, or how he may change the current of a lifetime of fixed habits of thought, speech, and action.[48]

Our study of Luke 10: 1–9 is found within the larger context of Jesus' *journey* to Jerusalem.[49] Even though Jesus orders His disciples to get going, they are actually already on the move. The recurrent themes of "traveling," "going up," or "on His way" are evident in this extended passage. Jesus is on the go.

The idea of a *journey* is considered a *literary device* that Luke uses to organize his narrative. It's an example for Jesus' disciples to understand the importance of seeing the Christian life as a *journey*.[50] If we embrace the Lord's challenge to take a lifelong *journey* by making disciples, we must keep moving so we can turn as the Holy Spirit leads. What does this look like in the life of a follower of Christ today?

**The *Journey* May Begin in Reverse**

In his powerful book, *The Servant as Leader,* Robert Greenleaf writes, "The ability to withdraw and reorient oneself, if only for a moment, presumes that one has learned the art of systematic neglect, to sort out the more important from the less important — and the important from the urgent — and attend to the more important, even though there may be penalties and censure for the neglect of something else … Pacing oneself by appropriate withdrawal is one of the best approaches to making optimal use of one's resources. The servant-as-leader must constantly ask himself, how can I use

---

[48] Sheldon, Charles Monroe (2012-05-12). *In His Steps* (p. 16). Kindle edition.

[49] Luke 9:51–19:27.

[50] Powell, Mark Allan. *Introducing the New Testament.* Published by Baker Academic, a division of Baker Publishing Group. © 2009. Used by permission.

myself to serve best?"[51]

Going in reverse is traveling backward while facing forward.

I cannot tell you how many times I've heard people say we need to go back to the altar, or go back to old-time religion, or go back to the way things used to be. Jesus isn't interested in going backward or back in time. He's moving us forward. He's pushing us toward eternity. He wants us to keep going. On the topic of looking back, C.S. Lewis writes:

> "Many religious people lament that the first fervors of their conversion have died away. They think — sometimes rightly, but not, I believe, always — that their sins account for this. They may even try by pitiful efforts of will to revive what now seem to have been the golden days. But were those fervors — the operative word is those — ever intended to last?"[52]

Are you following my thought here? Jesus is on the go. We cannot go backwards to find Him, because He has already moved on. However, we might need to go in reverse (while looking forward) to find the correct path.

> "It would be rash to say that there is any prayer which God never grants. But the strongest candidate is the prayer we might express in the single word *encore*. And how should the Infinite repeat himself? All space and time are too finite for Him to utter himself even once. And the joke — or tragedy — of it all is that these golden moments in the past, which are so tormenting if we erect them into a norm, are entirely nourishing, wholesome, and enchanting if we are content to

---

[51] Greenleaf, Robert (2012-07-10). *The Servant as Leader* (pp. 226-233). The Greenleaf Center for Servant Leadership.

[52] Lewis, C.S. *Letters to Malcolm* (p. 26-27). Orlando: Harcourt.

---

accept them for what they are: memories. Properly bedded down in a past which we do not miserably try to conjure back, they will send up exquisite growths. Leave the bulbs alone, and the new flowers will come up. Grub them up and hope, by fondling and sniffing, to get last year's blooms, and you will get nothing."[53]

## Jesus Says *Go,* Not *Come*

In today's Church, one of the favorite forms of evangelism is the passive invitation to visit for a service. This strategy has become our evangelistic baseline because it's hardly offensive, it's easy to execute, and it's simple to do without risk of being labeled a nut. But Jesus calls us to more than microwave evangelism. He calls us to boldly step outside our comfort zones and become proactive, going to where the people are, instead of waiting for them to come to us. Sadly, fewer unchurched individuals are visiting services. This means that Christians need to live out a missional, incarnational faith on a daily basis by *going*.

When Jesus tells His disciples to go, He is commanding them to take ground and move forward.

I have learned to love soccer, but most North Americans I know love gridiron football more than soccer. I asked a friend, who loves football, why this is so. He laughed and replied, "Americans love football because the objective is to take ground. America was founded and built on people taking ground. That's where the victory is."

Being a disciple of Jesus by going, is one of the most thrilling responsibilities you'll ever have. It's fraught with danger, the

---

[53] Ibid.

unknown, the untested, and the uncharted. It's a life assignment that will — at times — throw you into harm's way, where stress, discomfort, and sacrifice are the norms. But going will also will bring the greatest rewards, joys, and relationships you've ever known. Joil Marbut says it like this: "Your greatest encounter with God, your most effective ministry, your utmost satisfaction in life, is just one step outside your comfort zone."

Some people say you either go or send. I understand the idea, but in reality, Jesus calls all of us to go. After all, your mission field does not begin at the border; it begins at your skin. And we are all on a *journey* to go to places beyond our skin.

Most Christians are convinced that if we, the church at large, would move beyond the skin and take responsibility for the work of the ministry, the church could witness the greatest revival and harvest history has yet to witness. Sadly, however, it seems we continue relegating ministry, or at least certain elements of it, to a clergy or priestly class. A new reformation is within our reach if we could truly get our souls around Ephesians 4:12-13 and understand that ministry is the work of ALL believers. "Leaders in the community of faith are responsible to teach, train and equip the believers to do His work, the ministry, and to build up the church, the body of Christ. If we will have leaders who will equip, and believers who will minister, we will all come to great unity in our faith, grown in our knowledge of God and become mature in the Lord, being more like Jesus every day."[54]

There is a terrible cost to pay when the church fails to live out the priesthood of every believer. For in doing so we miss great opportunities to be uniquely used of the Holy Spirit. And secondly, we place unreal burdens on what we have classified as clergy. For that reason, too many ministers are

---

[54] My personal paraphrase of Ephesians 4:12-13.

halfway out the door, retiring posthaste, the spring gone out of their step.

"Despite denials, most ministers know deep inside they are not on top of their ministry; the ministry is on top of them. Ministers are leading churches that have lost touch with the texts, texture, and tensions of our times."[55] It is urgent that we all share the burden of discipleship and go as ones ministering the gospel.

This is an alarming call. All individuals have a place at the Church's evangelistic table, regardless of degrees they hold or lack, their profession, the street where they live, or the origin of their ancestors. God doesn't need professionals, the socially relevant, the rich, or the contemporary to carry out His will; He needs followers who are bent on going and doing His will no matter the cost.

The Church always needs to ensure that both clergy and laity are responsible to go and make disciples. Let's not fall into the trap of delegating the going to a chosen few who are ordained, licensed, or certified, or to a committee or department. It's an impossible task with eternal consequences, and the burden to make disciples is on every follower of Jesus Christ, not just those who minister for a living.

Please understand this is not a call for less than professional servanthood, an elimination of codes of conduct, or lack of recognition for called positions of leadership. An observation of the apostle Paul's organization of community life contains no detailed confession or code to subscribe to, no liturgical order to govern meetings, no clerical leadership to control matters. This does not mean that Paul was unconcerned

---

[55] Sweet, Leonard. *SoulTsunami: Sink or Swim in New Millennium Culture* (pp. 283-286). Zondervan.

---

about right belief and conduct, order, and decency in church, or stability and unity within and between communities. Nor does it mean that statements of faith, principles of conduct, criteria for assembling, distinctions between members, and tangible expressions of fellowship did not exist within them. Despite this apparent absence of all institutional means of support, *we should not imagine that Paul's work was provisional and incomplete.*[56] (Italics mine)

Many consider Martin Luther the father of today's evangelical faith. On Oct. 31, 1517, he defiantly nailed his 95 theses to the front door of the Wittenberg Castle Church in Germany. The bold move listed 95 reasons why the Catholic church and the pope were wrong and reformation was necessary. Luther's theses indeed caused a reformation that changed the history of Christianity and the world. From the Reformation came three sola: (Three Alones)

**Sola scriptura** (by Scripture alone) — the belief that Scripture trumps tradition.
**Sola fide** (by faith alone) — faith trumps works.
**Sola gratia** (by grace only) — grace trumps merit.

Another sola born out of the Reformation is sola sacerdos (the priesthood of the believer), which not only gives the layperson a right to go and make disciples, but gives him or her the responsibility to do so. If your church hasn't already, it's time to break down the wall that separates clergy and laity when it comes to making disciples. I am not suggesting that we rid our churches of pastors called to lead, or teachers called to instruct, or deacons called to serve. I am, however, calling for shared responsibility.

---

[56] Banks, Robert J. (1994-02-01). *Paul's Idea of Community: The Early House Churches in Their Cultural Setting*, revised edition (Kindle locations 3378-3383). Baker Book Group.

---

The benefits of this shared responsibility to go are profound. When we go, good things happen to those we disciple, our spiritual lives are enriched, the Church is strengthened and grows, and of course, heaven eventually becomes more populated.

## Going Is Therapeutic

When we don't go as we should, our spiritual muscles atrophy, and everyone loses across the heavenly boards.

Years ago, our church acquired an old building in downtown Cuenca, designed to house our first church in Ecuador. While removing debris after a rainstorm, I fell through the roof and snapped my wrist. Weeks later, a doctor removed my cast to reveal a shriveled forearm that had atrophied and become immobile.

I quizzed my physician about why this happened. The doctor explained that the immobility didn't result from breaking the bone or the length of time in the cast. Instead, the immobility occurred due to non-use while my wrist healed. When followers of Jesus are immobilized as in times of a healing process — or when nonprofessionals are delegated to do all the heavy lifting of evangelism and discipleship — mission atrophy sets in. When I look around the church, I believe I see many suffering from this illness. We could use some spiritual therapy!

Okay, we're on a roll, moving. Word Five, however, will point out that the *journey* does have some hidden dangers.

# S.T.O.P.

**Ponder the key word <u>Go</u> again and ask yourself the following questions:**

What was Jesus saying when he used the word <u>Go</u>?

What did Jesus want them to understand?

What does the word <u>Go</u> now mean to me?

What does Jesus want to convey to me through this word?

**Now let's live it out. How will you respond to what you have heard, read, learned, or felt inspired to do?**

S. SPECIFIC: What specifically will you do in response to the key word?

T. TIME-SENSITIVE: Within what time frame will you begin or complete the task?

O. OBTAINABLE: Is it possible? If not, go back to S.

P. PERTINENT: How does this goal relate to the key word <u>Go</u> and our understanding of it?

*Read It - Think It - Write It - Share It*

---

# 5

## Word Five – Wolves
### *Appreciated Anguish*

Key word: Wolves – metaphor of cruel, greedy, rapacious, destructive persons.[57]

Key verse: "I am sending you out like lambs among wolves" (Luke 10:3).

Key thought: Pain is part of the *journey*. Not pain for pain's sake, it's just an inevitable part of the process that we will one day, hopefully, appreciate.

———————

To understand the word wolves, we should first take a moment to look at a descriptive word Jesus uses to describe His disciples: lambs.

No less than 200 times does Scripture refer to followers of Jesus Christ as lambs or sheep. Seeing Christianity through a modern American lens, it seems difficult to understand the allegory.

———————

[57] Greek Lexicon. G3074 (KJV). *Blue Letter Bible.*

———

**Why Would He Call Us Lambs?**

Why not call His followers something more elegant, regal, beautiful, majestic, or strong? Something with marketability and moxie. Perhaps eagles, cheetahs, lions, or even cape buffaloes would suffice. No, Jesus chooses the lowly sheep. In Luke 10, Jesus reduces His followers even more by telling them to go as lambs. Is there an applicable message for today's disciple embedded in His short command?

By definition, a lamb is less than a year old. It hasn't reproduced and is small and weak enough to be easily devoured. Sheep are not the most intelligent animals. In fact, they seem mindless and content to be so — even to the point of death. "We all, like sheep, have gone astray, each of us has turned to our own way, and the Lord has laid on Him the iniquity of us all." (Isaiah 53:6)

Sheep are always the hunted, never the hunter. They have no claws, fangs, flying ability, camouflage techniques, evasive maneuvers, or defense mechanisms. When in danger, sheep panic and eventually die. So, why in the world would Jesus entrust such a monumental task — sharing His love and grace with a hostile world — to a bunch of lowly sheep? Perhaps He cares less about marketability and more about the strength found in weakness. The apostle Paul emphasizes this mission method when he records, "My grace is sufficient for you, for My power is made perfect in weakness. Therefore I will boast all the more gladly about my weaknesses, so that Christ's power may rest on me" (2 Corinthians 12:9).

The historian and gospel writer Luke punctuated the thought of weakness as well in his writings and is the only New

Testament author to mention Stephen's death. The martyrdom scene occurs quickly, in all of its brutality. [58]

## The Risk of Living Among <u>Wolves</u>

Eight hundred years after the New Testament writings, Eulogius of Cordoba, a Christian leader living among Muslims in Spain, called for a missiology of weakness and martyrdom. Eulogius lived his message, influencing many in the ways of Christ, and paid for it with his own sacrificial death. I am also reminded of the words of a young Quaker imprisoned on our own continent: "Here we are in prison on our own land for no crimes, no offense to God nor man; nay, more: we are here for obeying the commands of the Son of God and the influences of His Holy Spirit. I must look for patience in this dark day. I am troubled too much and excited and perplexed."[59] Cyrus Pringle knew firsthand that Christianity has always suffered more from those who have failed to understand the faith, than from those offended by it.[60]

The idea of Christians as weak sacrificial lambs has been the hallmark of the Church since its inception. The fresco paintings from the first century Roman catacombs show the Good Shepherd carrying a slain lamb or a sheep on His shoulders, plus two other sheep at his side.[61]

---

[58] Dollar, Harold. *St. Luke's Missiology: A Cross-cultural Challenge*, William Carey Library, 1996.

[59] Jones, Rufus, *The Record of a Quaker Conscience: Cyrus Pringle's Diary with an Introduction* by (Kindle locations 246-248). Kindle edition.

[60] Drummond, Henry. *Natural Law in the Spiritual World* (Kindle locations 832-833). Kindle edition.

[61] Hassett, M. (1910). The Lamb (in Early Christian Symbolism). In *The Catholic Encyclopedia*. New York: Robert Appleton Company.

---

Yet, not until the degeneration of Christian faith and practice during the times of Constantine the Great did the idea of militant evangelism take root, Leo Tolstoy notes. From that time forward, "These two ruling powers were constantly aiding one another to strive for nothing but outward glory. Divines and ecclesiastical dignitaries began to concern themselves only about subduing the whole world to their authority, incited men against one another to murder and plunder, and in creed and life reduced Christianity to a nullity."[62]

Tolstoy shows much alarm as he writes: "Christ, by means of His disciples, would have caught all the world in His net of faith, but the greater fishes broke the net and escaped out of it, and all the rest have slipped through the holes made by the greater fishes, so that the net has remained quite empty. The greater fishes who broke the net are the rulers, emperors, popes, kings, who have not renounced power, and instead of true Christianity have put on what is simply a mask of it."[63]

True sheep of the Good Shepherd, as portrayed in the ancient Roman frescoes, have no want or need to control or to lead. They are dependent animals content to follow, and they are uninterested in wielding power or controlling everything and everyone around them. In other words, they won't be the ones leading a team to victory. When Jesus called His followers sheep, He called them to follow Him unto death.

This goes against almost everything I have been taught about leading. Jesus, however, calls us to counterintuitive leadership. If He were in a boardroom, He'd tell His sheep to

[62] Tolstoy, Leo (2011-07-12). *The Kingdom of God Is Within You* (pp. 16-17). Kindle edition.
[63] Ibid., pp. 17-18.

lead by serving, submitting, and surrendering. That doesn't make sense in today's business world.

As leaders, we're supposed to have all the answers. We're supposed to bravely face our adversaries and never retreat. We're supposed to embrace risk with the confidence of highly paid CEOs.

If we're planting churches, we're supposed to go boldly into the unknown, and fake it until we make it. But Jesus' counterintuitive leadership strategy requires us to lead sans our strength, bravery, resolve, and selfish determination. Instead, we're supposed to rely solely on Him for supernatural interventions. By living out "Not by might or by power, but by my Spirit says the Lord," we truly become instruments in the hands of the living God.

In his play *Murder in the Cathedral*, T. S. Eliot describes a weak martyr as one "who has become an instrument of God, who has lost his will in the will of God, not lost it but found it, for he has found freedom in submission to God. The martyr no longer desires anything for himself, not even the glory of martyrdom."[64] J.R.R. Tolkien helps us understand that a quest is never a matter of one's own desire, but rather of one's calling.[65]

From the New Testament, it's easy to assume Jesus is more concerned with serving and submissiveness than leading. Through submissiveness and serving, however, Jesus teaches us some of the greatest lessons about leading.

---

[64] The Voice of the Martyrs (2002-01-01). *Extreme Devotion* (pp. 534-535). Thomas Nelson.
[65] Frost, Michael; Hirsch, Alan (2011-04-15). *The Faith of Leap, Embracing a Theology of Risk, Adventure & Courage* (Shapevine) (pp. 174-175). Baker Publishing Group.

---

The servant leader is servant first. It begins with the natural feeling that one wants to serve above all else. Then, conscious choice brings one to aspire to lead.

That person is sharply different from one who is leader first, perhaps because of the need to assuage an unusual power drive or to acquire material possessions. The *leader first* and the *servant first* are two extreme types. Between them, there are shadings and blends that are part of the infinite variety of human nature. The difference manifests itself in the care taken by the *servant first* to make sure that other people's highest priority needs are being served. Do those being served grow as persons? Do they become healthier, wiser, freer, more autonomous? What is the impact on the least privileged in society? Will they benefit or at least not be further deprived? And by all means may we not be the ones to confirm the words of Brennan Manning, "The institutional church has become a wounder of the healers rather than a healer of the wounded."[66]

As a "Professional Ordained Clergyman," I have found myself swinging on the pendulum between these two positions, Servant First and Leader First. I have been abused and I have abused. I have hurt others and others have hurt me. Does this just come with the territory?

Let me offer a few thoughts for insight:

- Most of my regrets and mistakes have come when living the Leader First style.

- The want for power and the need to control is, in my opinion, the greatest sin and mistake of today's evangelical leadership.

---

[66] Manning, Brennan. *The Ragamuffin Gospel: Good News for the Bedraggled, Beat-Up, and Burnt Out* (p. 16). The Crown Publishing Group.

---

- John Bueno, former Executive Director of Assemblies of God World Mission, often said, "If we are going to err, let's err on the side of grace." And after all, did Jesus not die wounded, abused and taken advantage of?

- Regardless of the pains that come from *both* leading and serving, let us not be robbed of our joy, ministry, servanthood, or leadership by what I call the "Big Cs" — Cynical, Callous, Critical, Cruddy, Corny, Coldhearted, Crampy, Contemptuous, and Condescending. Life is too wonderful and short to live otherwise.

## Our One Gift

Jesus calls His sheep to bring nothing as a sacrifice other than themselves. That in itself is an amazing task and a completely risky leadership strategy in today's world. But Jesus is undaunted. Think of it. Jesus is admitting that His followers — the lowly sheep — do not have the strength to plow, nor the frame to carry a burden, nor the will to lead. Instead, they're merely called to serve others to the point of death. Try selling that strategy to a roomful of CEOs or church leaders bent on going and making disciples in dangerous mission fields. We probably should be less worried about <u>wolves</u> in sheepskins, and more concerned about sheep in wolf skins.

Still, Jesus persists. If He has His way, His sheep will bring themselves in service to Him, their Shepherd. They'll have no middleman, carry no encumbrance, and no longer lean on their own experience, talents, or special skills. None of it makes sense until we turn to a famous Psalm:

"The Lord is my shepherd, I lack nothing. He makes

———

me lie down in green pastures, He leads me beside quiet waters, He refreshes my soul. He guides me along the right paths for His name's sake. Even though I walk through the darkest valley, I will fear no evil, for You are with me; Your rod and Your staff, they comfort me.

"You prepare a table before me in the presence of my enemies. You anoint my head with oil; my cup overflows. Surely Your goodness and love will follow me all the days of my life, and I will dwell in the house of the Lord forever" (Psalm 23:1-6).

Certainly this flies in the face of everything the world tells us about being strong, able, and great. Our large institutions need larger-than-life leaders. Magnificent stadiums need the best athletes. Successful corporations need brilliant CEOs. But the Great Shepherd needs only lowly sheep — sheep that listen and follow — to accomplish His will on earth. They must be broken men and women completely submissive to the Cross.

That sets the stage for our key word, <u>wolves</u>. Want to be a martyr? The <u>wolves</u> are at your service.

In January 1956, missionaries Jim Elliot, Ed McCully, Peter Fleming, Roger Youderian, and Nate Saint landed their Missionary Aviation Fellowship plane on a tiny patch of sand deep in Ecuador's interior. In the weeks leading up to the landing, the missionaries had made contact — and had even air-dropped gifts — for a tribe known by outsiders as the Aucas, although they called themselves the Waoranis. Though the Waoranis had a reputation for unprovoked killing sprees, the missionaries felt called to risk their faith and fate with them.

There is little growth or reward in life without taking risks. As a parable says, the one who buried his treasure in the ground did so to avoid risk of loss, failure, and disapproval. In the end, though, he reaped all three of these disasters. Clearly, avoidance of risk is the greatest risk of all.[67]

And we are not talking about a risk just for risk's sake, for "faith is not belief without proof, but is trust without reservation." Faith is more an act of courage than it is an act of knowledge.[68]

The determination of five young missionaries to share the gospel, despite the inherent risks, proved fatal. Everyone died at the end of a Waorani spear. They showed you cannot build God's reputation if you aren't willing to risk your own.[69]

Living among wolves, no matter how noble the cause, is something your brain won't like. Your brain has more than 100 billion nerves that communicate in trillions of connections called synapses that keep us breathing, thinking, reacting, and living.[70] That last point — living — runs in direct contradiction to being among wolves.

God hardwired your brain to implore you to fight or take flight when danger appears. In other words, your brain is bent on self-preservation. So, when you willingly throw yourself among the wolves as Nate Saint and his colleagues

[67] Cloud, Henry (2007-09-11). *9 Things You Simply Must Do to Succeed in Love and Life: A Psychologist Learns from His Patients What Really Works and What Doesn't* (p. 36). Thomas Nelson.

[68] Frost, Michael; Hirsch, Alan (2011-04-15). *The Faith of Leap: Embracing a Theology of Risk, Adventure & Courage* (Shapevine) (Kindle locations 1231-1232). Baker Publishing Group.

[69] Batterson, Mark (2011-12-20). *The Circle Maker: Praying Circles Around Your Biggest Dreams and Greatest Fears* (p. 46). Zondervan.

[70] Mastin, Luke. (2010) *www.human-memory.net/brain_neurons.html*.

did, your brain is going to retaliate. It's going to tell you that what you're doing does not make any sense.

It will shout: *That's not safe!* It will reason: *Someone else can do it.* It will implore: *We're not crazy; let's go where it's safe!* Simultaneously, your memory, which is located deep in your temporal lobe, likely will drudge up some compelling data to support any notion you may have to stay among the <u>wolves</u>.
Look at Jesus' disciples. Almost all of them died horrible martyr deaths. We don't want to go through that, do we? However, a life lived in fear is a life half lived. Likewise, a church addicted to security and safety is not the Church of Jesus Christ.[71] Quite simply, it is something else entirely: "Greater love has no one than this: to lay down one's life for one's friends."[72]

God gave us brains, and they are wonderfully made to help us make good decisions that can save our lives. But God also called us to live among <u>wolves</u>. Dietrich Bonhoeffer describes this idea well in his classic work, *The Cost of Discipleship*:

> "The cross is laid on every Christian. The first Christ-suffering which every man must experience is the call to abandon the attachments of this world. It is that dying of the 'old man' which is the result of his encounter with Christ. As we embark upon discipleship we surrender ourselves to Christ in union with his death — we give over our lives to death. Thus it begins; the Cross is not the terrible end to an otherwise God-fearing and happy life, but it meets us

---

[71] Frost, Michael; Hirsch, Alan (2011-04-15). *The Faith of Leap, Embracing a Theology of Risk, Adventure & Courage* (Shapevine) (Kindle locations 666-668). Baker Publishing Group.
[72] John 15:13.

---

at the beginning of our communion with Christ. When Christ calls a man, he bids him come and die."[73]

Bonhoeffer undoubtedly felt inspired by Early Church fathers who declared that the call, rather than the suffering, made genuine martyrs.[74]

It's not a sacrifice for sacrifice's sake, for one can give everything one owns for a cause. But if the cause is self-serving, superficial, or carnal, the sacrifice will leave you as empty as anything the world has to offer. Jesus said He came to give us life, and life to its fullest. That fullness can be found in sacrificing one's self through love that impacts the lives of others.

## A Radical and Sacrificial Gift

Know this: When we go, we go to die. That certainly qualifies as a different kind of going; it is a going that finds its call in tough, radical, sacrificial love.

> "Love is patient, love is kind. It does not envy, it does not boast, it is not proud. It does not dishonor others, it is not self-seeking, it is not easily angered, it keeps no record of wrongs. Love does not delight in evil but rejoices with the truth. It always protects, always trusts, always hopes, always perseveres" (1 Corinthians 13:4-7).

---

[73] Bonhoeffer, Dietrich. *The Cost of Discipleship* (p. 99) New York: Touchstone, 1995.
[74] The Voice of the Martyrs. (2002-01-01). *Extreme Devotion* (pp. 508-509). Thomas Nelson.

---

Many times, we treat love as passive, submissive, warm, and fuzzy. It's anything but that when we *go*. As I read Paul's aforementioned description of love, one word stands out to me more than the others: *perseveres*. Other translations use the word *endures*. It's the kind of persistent love that responds to Christ's invitation: "Whoever does not take up their cross and follow Me is not worthy of Me. Whoever finds their life will lose it, and whoever loses their life for My sake will find it" (Matthew 10:38, 39).

Radical, tough love compels us to sacrifice our own well-being for the well-being of others. In his "I've Been to the Mountaintop" speech the day before his assassination, Martin Luther King Jr. taught with much clarity when analyzing the story of the Good Samaritan.

> "The first question that the priest asked, the first question that the Levite asked was, 'If I stop to help this man, what will happen to me?' But then the Good Samaritan came by, and he reversed the question: 'If I do not stop to help this man, what will happen to him?'"[75]

Radical, tough, and sacrificial love does not throw caution to the wind, but it does throw the one who practices it into harm's way. To be sure, there will be costs to be counted, calculated, and evaluated. God doesn't mince words when He talks about the price and risk of going. You may very well have to pay the ultimate price. Everyone around you may have to pay a steep price. Your family, friends, reputation, finances, and social status may all be impacted.

Yes, the costs are real. Yes, you will have to sacrifice and risk much for others to become disciples of Christ. Yes, you will

---

[75] King, Martin Luther, Jr., *"I've Been to the Mountaintop."* April 3, 1968.

see God work miracles through your life and ministry. Yes, you will pay the price. But the rewards are as real as the costs. This we can never forget.

Wolves are scary encounters. Taking no money on the *journey* can be just as scary. Chapter 6 might be a bigger fright yet.

# S.T.O.P.

**Consider the key word <u>Wolves</u> again and ask yourself the following questions:**

What was Jesus saying to His disciples through the use of this term?

What did Jesus want them to understand?

What does the word <u>Wolves</u> now mean to me?

What does Jesus want to convey to me through this word?

**Now let's live it out. How will you respond to what you have heard, read, learned, or felt inspired to do?**

S. SPECIFIC: What specifically will you do in response to the word <u>Wolves</u>?

T. TIME-SENSITIVE: Within what time frame will you begin or complete the task?

O. OBTAINABLE: Is it possible? If not, go back to S.

P. PERTINENT: How does this goal relate to the key word and our understanding of it?

*Read It - Think It - Write It - Share It*

# PART THREE
## *Don't the Don'ts*

Key words six, seven and eight: Purse – Sandals – Greet

As great teachers do, Jesus begins with the dos, and now He discusses the don'ts.

At first glance, you might think that these are just poetic words to fill in the discourse. However, I believe you will find they are important stepping stones to successful discipleship.

### Flawless Daunt

She had been told by more than one breath
that following such paths would lead to death
her stubbornness lead by flawless daunt
took her quickly to the place of no want.
—W.E.M.

# 6

## Word Six – <u>Purse</u>
### *Cashless Capital*

Key word: <u>Purse</u> – a money bag[76]

Key verse: "Do not take a <u>purse</u>…" (Luke 10:4).

Key thought: Some activities are priceless, some can be cashless, but the *journey* is made up of both. Some of the most effective work of the Kingdom needs no cash, just a lot of capital.

––––––––––

The Scriptures, both the Old and New Testaments, say that the raven is fed by its Creator, and He provides for the bird's every need. Isn't it interesting, then, that when Elijah comes to one of life's impossible situations, a raven is God's instrument of provision? Elijah believed the Word of the Lord and banished himself to the cutoff lands of the Kerith Ravine.

For God had promised, "You will drink from the brook, and I have directed the ravens to supply you with food there." So, Elijah obeyed and, as promised, "The ravens brought him bread and meat in the morning and bread and meat in the evening, and he drank from the brook" (1 Kings 17:4-6).

––––––––––

[76] Greek Lexicon. G905 (KJV), *Blue Letter Bible*.

––

Divine intervention, against overwhelming odds, is a repeated theme in Scripture. And for that reason, Jesus teaches His followers that their hope and provision are in Him. They learn through experience that their dependence and hope come from the Lord, their Jehovah Jireh, and Provider of all.

Our prayers and trust in God release His provision, but on His time frame, not ours. The waiting, seeking, asking, patience, the moments of true trust and dependence — waiting for *Him* to show up — are what mature us the most in life.[77] Even in the dark times, we will experience His caring, compassionate love and timely intervention. We learn to turn to the One who provides all, and He will not let us down. We do so, just as Elijah obeyed God's commands. The prophet drank water from a brook and ate bread and meat brought by ravens. Everything is under the Lord's command.[78]

Yet, we have all experienced that within our hearts is a "tough, fibrous, and fallen root whose nature is always to *possess*. It covets with a deep and fierce passion," writes A.W. Tozer. We constantly use the simple words *my* and *mine* as if we were still young children. The use of these pronouns seems innocent when written, but their constant use is significant. "They express the real nature of the old Adamic man better than a thousand volumes of theology could do. They are verbal symptoms of our deep disease," Tozer adds. Could it be that these gifts of God, now take the place of God Himself?[79] And then, to add strength to this 'disease,' does our culture not associate economic prosperity with happiness?

---

[77] Scripture In Use. *Essential 50 Biblical Stories*, (2017-06-06)
*http://www.scripturesinuse.org/gods-provision-perfect-timing*. Classic Bridges.
[78] Ibid.
[79] Tozer, A. W. *The Pursuit of God*, (Chapter 2 ). World Invisible.

We can agree that an increase of economic output can lead to upturns in the standard of living, but that does NOT guarantee an increase in human happiness and satisfaction. "Much of modern life is based upon a false logic that assumes happiness and well-being come from financial prosperity."[80]

Studies show that many countries, such as our own, have had substantial economic growth in recent decades, yet national satisfaction and happiness has had no noticeable growth.

Have we allowed ourselves to believe that bigger purses will bring greater contentment and satisfaction? [81] When Jesus says to take "no purse," perhaps the lesson is clear; money and Kingdom sometimes have very little in common. Let us not assume that money is the answer to every Kingdom need and goal.

## A Bag

In the time of Christ, a purse was a bag for money. Travelers, when on a *journey*, usually carried this special purse or bag, in which they protected their currency. Connie carries a purse wherever she goes. (I remember my grandmother calling her purse a handbag.) It's quite different from the days of the New Testament.

Connie's purse transports cash, a couple of credit cards, makeup, a pen, a small first-aid kit, travel sewing kit, some mints, and anything else she'd need for a two-week stint on *Survivor.*

---

[80] Marks, Nic. *The Happiness Manifesto* (Kindle single) (TED Books) (Kindle locations 158-163). TED Books.
[81] scribd. (2016-12-10)
www.scribd.com/document/56474440/GDP-Growth-is-No-Measure-of-Societal-Progress.

I'd never even think of asking her to travel — let alone leave our house — without her purse. It's an essential possession that has bailed us out of many dilemmas. But Jesus didn't hesitate to ask His disciples to go without purses.

On the surface, this is a strange command, but He wanted to make a deeper point. The purse — money really — can easily become a replacement for creative problem solving and, more importantly, dependency on God. In his book *The Upside-Down Kingdom*, Donald B. Kraybill writes that the values and norms of society have become so deeply ingrained in our way of thinking that we find it almost impossible to consider unconventional alternatives.

Alcoholics Anonymous is credited with the recovery of more alcoholics from that dreadful illness than all other approaches combined. The founding meeting to incorporate the organization took place in the office of a noted wealthy philanthropist. In the course of the meeting, money came up as a topic of discussion. Ultimately, leaders resolved that the work of AA cannot be carried out primarily as a revenue generator. These principles have guided the work of AA over the years. No one but an alcoholic can contribute money to the Alcoholics Anonymous modest budget; AA will own no real property; the essential work of AA — one recovered (or recovering) alcoholic helping another toward recovery — won't involve the exchange of money.

What if the Church followed similar direction when it comes to church planting and discipleship? In many communities where the evangelical church has yet to be established, AA is alive and well. Maybe the cashless capital plan is more effective than we realize.

"Jesus presented the kingdom of God as a new paradigm, new wineskins. Jesus overturned the old methods, values, and

---

96

ideologies. As kingdom citizens, we can't assume that things are right just because that's the way they are. The upside-down perspective focuses the points of difference between God's kingdom and the kingdoms of the world."[82]

## Money Follows Obedience

One of my friends commonly asks people who say they want to accomplish great deeds for God — but aren't doing them — what they would be doing for Him if money didn't enter the equation. Every time I've heard him ask this, the person he's talking to relates their big plans with vigor and wide eyes. As I listen, I always think these are the kinds of plans that have no limits. They're grand schemes on a grand scale. Indeed, they are the kind of dreams God wants us to dream. But inevitably, the person replies, "If I only had the money, I'd do it." To which my friend always says, "Money follows obedience."

The problem is that most of us don't follow through on chasing the vision God has set for us. So we never discover if the money really does follow obedience. That's a shame. If Jesus tells us to go without a purse, He's telling us that He'll take care of our needs and all the details. He's asking us to depend solely on Him instead of on earthly provisions. Sure, going without a purse requires great faith, but that's the point.

We're seemingly thrown another curveball later in Luke 22:36, when Jesus tells His disciples to carry a wallet for the *journey*: "If you have a purse, take it, and also a bag; and if you don't have a sword, sell your cloak and buy one." Did Jesus

---

[82] Kraybill, Donald B. (2012-11-21). *The Upside-Down Kingdom* (pp. 180-181). Herald Press.

have a change of heart? No. In Luke 10, He establishes the idea that we need to be completely dependent on Him and His provision. In Luke 22, He's teaching the disciples, and us, to use the resources we have to do the work He needs to have done. He is not calling us to be rich or to be comfortable, although that is a wonderful blessing from the Lord. He is calling us to die to ourselves so that others might know Him. To be sure, Jesus isn't asking us to do anything He didn't do.[83] Jesus borrowed a womb to be born, a boat to preach from, a donkey to ride on, a boy's lunch to feed the multitude, and even a room for the Last Supper. Aside from that, the Son of Man had nowhere to lay His head.[84] Maybe the Anabaptists are right when they suggest that the frequent association of the Church with status, wealth, and force is inappropriate for followers of Jesus, and it damages our witness.[85]

Some time back, I celebrated a wedding in a rural Quechua community. About 100 people attended, and all stayed for dinner. As I looked around the tables, I realized that I knew everyone in attendance, and everyone was a believer.

What really astounded me, though, was that I had only led one person in the room to faith in Jesus Christ. And that disciple, Juan, had shared his newfound faith and made disciples of dozens of others.

Actually, every person in that room could trace their spiritual heritage back to Juan. Playing a small part in those lives didn't cost me a penny. I did, however, dip into my cashless capital. The investment will no doubt pay eternal dividends.

---

[83] Christoyannopoulos, Alexandre. (pp. 109-110) *Christian Anarchism: A Political Commentary on the Gospel.* Exeter: Imprint Academic.
[84] Luke 9:58.
[85] Core Beliefs – The Official Blog of Benjamin L. Corey.

Jesus' discipleship *journey* highlights the fact that money can never compete with obedience.

Here's something disturbing to consider. In 2016, Americans reported giving $125 billion to religious organizations.[86] With billions donated annually, why have hundreds of millions of people still not heard of the saving grace of Jesus Christ?

I can't help but think that somewhere along the way we — as the Church — have prioritized giving to the point that we have provided a great excuse and replacement for going and making disciples. Jesus makes it clear that money is part of the process. But it should never replace going and making disciples. The command to give can never replace the command to go.

It's time to change the equation. It's time to go. It's time to make disciples. It's time to transform lives by sharing Christ's message of love and grace, no matter how much or how little money we have in our purses.

Now that you're comfortable with the idea of going without financial backing, you need to grow accustomed to going without your luggage. "Don't take a traveler's bag with you,"[87] Jesus commanded.

On July 27, 1974, Connie, 17 at the time, and I, 20, loaded everything we owned into a 1966 Volkswagen Beetle that Connie's dad had rebuilt and given to us as a wedding present. After saying goodbye to our families, I pressed the pedal to the *very thin* metal as we basked in the thought of our bright future. We couldn't have been happier. Nine hundred miles and 18 hours later, we arrived in Lakeland, Florida, for

---

[86] Giving USA. *Total Charitable Donations Rise to New High of $390.05 Billion*, June 12, 2017.
[87] Luke 10:4 (my modification).

—

a one-of-a-kind honeymoon that would end with us enrolling in Bible college.

We must have been nuts. Everything we owned fit in the back of a Beetle. We had very little money. No job prospects. No place to call our own, yet I still felt extremely confident as we drove toward our future. Now, more than 40 years later, I sometimes find myself wishing I had the same fortitude and optimism as the 20-year-old kid who drove full steam ahead toward Lakeland with his new bride.

Was it simply youthful vigor fueling my pursuit of our future? Or just my need for adventure? Or something else? I'll never be sure, but in retrospect we had this going for us:

- We had nothing to lose — or at least we lived as though we had nothing to lose.

- We made ourselves available to go where God directed.

- We had no debt.

- We showed more interest in accumulating experiences than possessions.

- We owned few worldly possessions.

As I write this, I am reminded of Mark Twain's story, *The Prince and the Pauper*. The little prince contemplated the little pauper gravely a moment, then said:

> *"And prithee, why not? Who helpeth them undress at night? Who attireth them when they rise?"*
> *"None, sir. Would'st have them take off their garment, and sleep without —like the beasts?"*
> *"Their garment! Have they but one?"*

*"Ah, good your worship, what would they do with more? Truly they have not two bodies each."* [88]

Our lack of stuff afforded us mobility that we've strived for ever since. Our lack of stuff empowered us to chase God's will for our lives. Our lack of stuff made us feel as if we had nothing to lose. Our lack of stuff emboldened us and made us feel brave.

But, along with most people, we're always drawn to the stuff. And as those belongings accumulate, we start reaching for luggage to haul it around. Time and time again we've found ourselves lugging our possessions through the chapters of life. In most cases, that luggage has added more weight than value. I can't help but wonder if that is why Jesus told the disciples not to take a bag (luggage) when He told them to go and make disciples.

Take no bag. In other words, travel light, because going and discipling others is easier sans the luggage of life, whether you're an individual or a church.

Like churches, sometimes we — no matter how simply we're trying to live — can't help pulling luggage into the equation of our lives and ministries. For instance, every time I've ever discussed church planting, evangelism, or even worker training, mapping, planning, or goal setting, someone inevitably brings up buildings, land, equipment, or the lack of such necessities.

Being strategic and thinking through our needs isn't bad, but dwelling on all the things we will need before we are willing to go and make disciples is unacceptable, for both the Church and individuals.

---

[88] Twain, Mark. *The Prince and the Pauper*, (Chapter 3) Creative Commons.

In Luke 10, it's as if Jesus is testing His disciples by challenging them to go and make disciples without the luggage to which they are addicted. He's telling them plainly that He's more than prepared to provide for their every need — if they'll trust Him to provide. I can imagine the conversation He might have had with His disciples after they first went out.

"When I sent you without purse, bag, or sandals, did you lack anything?" "No, nothing," they answered. "We had all we needed." "Exactly!" "But, Lord, we can't always depend on this. Well, can we?"

Yes, we can depend on Him. Here's why. God wants His kingdom filled with His followers more than we do. Because of that, He frees up our movements to expedite the evangelism and discipleship process if we are willing to live without the trappings of our luggage.

When we live a "luggage-less life," we're free to make personal connections with those who don't know Jesus. We're free to move. We're free to go. Think of this: God designed us to connect with one another so that the Good News will spread and stick.

That requires us to make building and fostering relationships with others the priority of our lives. Yes, people may come to our churches for the innovative buildings, the entertaining services, and top-tier programs, but they'll only stay if they feel truly connected with others.

Sometimes that simple truth gets lost in our desire to do good work for God. I know this from experience.

# Bellboy

A few years ago, Connie and I led our congregation through a building program, discipleship classes, and a couple of new church plants. I felt certain everything I did fostered evangelism and discipleship. In hindsight, I can't honestly claim that.

During those frenzied days of growth, I collected luggage like a bellboy. I wanted others to recognize me and the work I accomplished. My ego and track record of success had given me an edge of arrogance that I knew didn't come from God. Every day stress ate at me from the inside out. A force pushed me to work around the clock and to drive my teams to do better at every turn.

Without a doubt, I had allowed the luggage of life, church, success, and my own blind spots to sidetrack me from God's will. During that time I was not as effective, pleasant, caring, graceful, patient, kind, or loving as I should have been. Sure, I desired to build something great for God. However, somewhere along the way, His kingdom took a backseat to my personal empire of stuff and power.

Even though I had allowed myself to be duped, God intervened through the words and actions of Connie, my staff, and colleagues. Each of them reminded me that my job was only to go and make disciples. In due time, with the gentleness that only God can bring to a situation, He hit the reset button on me and the projects on which I worked. Consequently, I became a lousy Bellboy. I ditched a lot of the luggage and returned to the liberty of doing His will like I had at age 20.

Our ministry benefited, as did I. I promised then to never let the luggage of life, expectations, or ego pull me off the mark of going and making disciples of Jesus. That has been the greatest lesson I've ever learned in four decades of ministry.

The luggage-less life is one solely dependent on God, His grace, and His provision. Such a life can seem extremely perilous, but I've never felt more at peace or comforted than when God was my sole Provider and I was empty-handed, freed from the things of this world.

### The Tyranny of Things
*by Elizabeth Morris*

*Once upon a time, when I was very tired, I chanced to go away to a little house by the sea. "It is empty," they said, "but you can easily furnish it." Empty! Yes, thank Heaven! Furnish it? Heaven forbid! Its floors were bare, its walls were bare, its tables, there were only two in the house, were bare. There was nothing in the closets but books; nothing in the bureau drawers but the smell of clean, fresh wood; nothing in the kitchen but an oil stove, and a few a very few dishes; nothing in the attic but rafters and sunshine, and a view of the sea. After I had been there an hour, there descended upon me a great peace, a sense of freedom, of infinite leisure. In the twilight I sat before the flickering embers of the open fire, and looked out through the open door to the sea, and asked myself, "Why?" Then the answer came: I was emancipated from things.*

How about emancipation from some of our shoes? More about that subject in the next chapter.

# S.T.O.P.

**Consider the key word <u>Purse</u> again and ask yourself the following questions:**

What was Jesus conveying to His disciples through the use of this word?

What did Jesus want them to understand by using the word <u>Purse?</u>

What does this word now mean to me?

What does Jesus want to convey to me through the phrase, "Take no purse"?

**Now let's live it out. How will you respond to what you have heard, read, learned, or felt inspired to do?**

S. SPECIFIC: What specifically will you do in response to the word <u>Purse?</u>

T. TIME-SENSITIVE: Within what time frame will you begin or complete the task?

O. OBTAINABLE: Is it possible? If not, go back to S.

P. PERTINENT: How does this goal relate to the key word and our understanding of it?

*Read It - Think It - Write It - Share It*

---

# 7

## Word Seven – Sandals
### *Sticky Stops*

Key word: Sandals – What is bound under, a sandal, a sole fastened to the foot with thongs[89]

Key verse: "Do not take a purse or bag or sandals..." (Luke 10:4).

Key thought: The *journey* is about finding those places where we can stop long enough to gather others for the trip.

———————

How many pairs of footwear do you own? If you're like most Americans, you own at least 20 pairs of shoes.[90] Twenty! Seeing that number in black and white almost feels shameful. But indeed, many of us own even more than that. We have our shoes and boots for myriad activities: running, tennis, lawn, pool, soccer, basketball, hiking, snow, walking and gardening. We wear dress shoes and high heels. (Well, not all of us wear high heels!)

Jesus said, "Do not take any sandals." What in the world has that to do with missions and discipleship?

———————————————

[89] Greek Lexicon. G5266 (KJV), *Blue Letter Bible.*
[90] TIME. (2006-03-05) *Style and Design Poll,*
*http://content.time.com/time/arts/article/0,8599,1169863,00.html.* Time.

———

Straight up I am giving a disclaimer: I might be completely mistaken in my interpretation of Jesus's command "Do not take any sandals." However, could it be that Jesus says to take no extra sandals because you won't be wearing them out, because mission and discipleship are more about staying than traveling? Whether this is Jesus' point or not, the message appears to be about staying, because He makes it quite clear that we are "not to move from house to house." (Luke 10:7)

I've had the opportunity to visit with many individuals interested, excited, enticed, and perhaps even called to serve in foreign missions. I cannot tell you how many times I've heard, "I think I'm called to missions because I love to travel." That always makes me smile. Feeling called to missions because one likes to travel is like saying, "I feel called to be a writer because I love to read."

## Missions Is Less About Traveling, More About Staying

You might be wondering, "I thought you said that this is a *journey*, now you are saying it's not about traveling, but rather *staying*." Well, actually both ideas are correct. The process of making disciples requires that we are on the move, GOING to destinations, to other people. We are required however to stop and stay long enough to prepare others for their *journey*.

From my experience, those who love to travel usually aren't the ones called to be missionaries. Traveling is only one aspect of missional living, albeit one of the most exciting and therefore most alluring. And deceptive.

Living missionally is an incredible, exciting way to serve God, but every opportunity comes with trade-offs. The trade-offs Jesus describes to His disciples include potential poverty, death to one's interests, sole reliance on His intervention and provision, and a life lived for the purpose of sharing Christ's message of love, grace, and peace.

Jesus told His disciples, "You will be hated by everyone because of Me, but the one who stands firm to the end will be saved" (Matthew 10:22). This mission doesn't sound like a job for a wide-eyed tourist who loves business class, gourmet meals, and seeing the world from the balconies of five-star hotels. Oh, how I love to travel tourist class, but this is a job for someone who would be content to travel the world with only one pair of sandals.

**Persistence**

More than a decade ago, Anders Ericsson and his colleagues at Berlin's elite Academy of Music conducted a study with musicians. With the help of professors, they divided violinists into three groups: world-class soloists, extremely competent violinists, and those without enough skills to play professionally. All of them started playing at roughly the same age and practiced about the same amount of time until the age of 8. That is when their practice habits diverged.

The researchers found that by the age of 20, the average players had logged about 4,000 hours of practice time, the really good violinists totaled about 8,000 hours, and the elite performers set the bar high with 10,000 hours.

While there is no denying that innate ability dictates some of a person's potential, that potential is only tapped via persistent effort.

Persistence is the magic bullet, and 10,000 hours seems to be the threshold to greatness. Tenacity, persistence, and doggedness are key to living out the *journey*.[91]

Colonel Harland Sanders, founder of Kentucky Fried Chicken, was a member of our home church in Louisville. Over the years, I came to know his story well. At age 65, he received his first Social Security check and was disappointed that the amount he received was only a few dollars north of a hundred. Instead of whining and complaining, the colonel used his disillusionment as motivation to sell his "finger-lickin' good" secret fried chicken recipe to restaurant owners throughout the nation.

With only a hundred bucks in his pocket, he set out across the U.S. wearing his trademark white suit and black bow tie. I can't help but believe that the colonel would have qualified and embraced the trade-offs Jesus offered His disciples when He told them to go.

Sanders traveled the country and, at the same time, he was sticking to his plan. He wasn't afraid to make a deal. In exchange for his secret recipe, he only asked for a small percentage of sales from each restaurateur who wanted to sell his chicken. At first, no one would even entertain his offer. With finances running thin, he saved money by sleeping in his car, scrimping on meals, and not spending even a penny unnecessarily.

The results of his hard work and sacrifices? Absolutely nothing.

His first visit with a potential client yielded no sales. Nor did the next nine pitches.

---

[91] Watchmen on The Wall. (2017-05-17).
*http://www.frc.org/prayerteam/prayer-targets-batterson-pastors-briefing-us-promoting-life-barna-nc-fake-news-trump-taps-frc*

The trend continued. Regardless of his sacrifices, determination, and passion, no one was willing to take his offer. I've known such realities, too, as a missionary. But the colonel persisted, persevered, and parked on his idea of selling his secret recipe in exchange for a small percentage of sales.

After visiting a thousand businesses, any normal person would have given up. Not the colonel! He took failure in stride, learned from it, kept his eyes on a greater prize, and eventually had a break. Business owner number 1,010 signed a contract with Sanders, launching KFC on its way to becoming one of the world's largest fast-food chains.

Maybe Jesus told His disciples to take only one pair of sandals because doing so speaks profoundly of staying, persistence, and perseverance. Perhaps Jesus wanted His disciples to be resolute and determined — like the colonel — so that regardless of the challenges, setbacks, failures, detours, and hurt, they would have staying power, resolve, and the ability to forge on. Or maybe Jesus knew that when their sandals wore out, His disciples would have no one else to provide for them other than Him.

There have been times when I have wanted to quit, run, hide, or abandon the course God set for Connie and me. I can recall dozens of moments when I wanted to give up. No doubt we could have easily blown through thousands of dollars catching the next flight out. But we didn't. We stayed, though not always valiantly.

I came home after one terribly discouraging experience. In my self-pity I moaned, "I'm done; we're leaving! This isn't worth it anymore."

Connie, in her quiet and steady manner, replied, "That's fine

Billy, but don't talk about going anywhere until God talks to you about going somewhere."

It wasn't until that moment that I understood that, when God calls us, He does not revoke the call just because circumstances get difficult, we run out of money, have no place to live, or face persecution. Fellow missionary and friend Dick Brogden once described the cost of going and discipling others succinctly and frankly, in a very unmarketable way.

> "Labors, stripes, prison, death, lashes, rods, stonings, shipwrecks, perils of waters, robbers, in the wilderness, false brethren, weariness, toil, sleeplessness, cold, naked,[92] tribulations, distress, imprisonment, tumults, dishonor, unknown, dying, chastening, sorrowful, poverty, having nothing,[93] hard pressed on every side, perplexed, persecuted, struck down, delivered to death for Jesus' sake,[94] trials of mocking, scourging, chains, imprisonment, stoned, sawn in two, tempted, slain with sword, tormented,[95] crucified with Christ,[96] bound in the Spirit, chains in Christ, to die is gain."

You get the idea. To go and make disciples of others is a call to sacrifice. It's a call to be persistent. It's a call to persevere through thick and thin. Though the *journey* will be fraught with danger, challenges, and peril, one pair of sandals is sufficient. Our fuel for such sacrifice is no further than the looks in the faces of our family and friends who do not know Jesus as their Savior.

---

[92] 2 Corinthians 11:23-27.
[93] 2 Corinthians 6:4-10.
[94] 2 Corinthians 4:8-12.
[95] Hebrews 11:36-40.
[96] Galatians 2:20.

The Bible shows that perseverance is one of the virtues expected of Christians.

It is proof of the genuineness of faith and spiritual maturity (John 8:31; Acts 14:22; Romans 5:3-4; Colossians 1:21-23; Hebrews 3:12-14; 4:1-11; 6:11-12). Persistence and faithful service are how God advances His kingdom.

The elements involved in perseverance, or steadfastness and persistence, are:

Spiritual growth (Ephesians 4:15)
Fruitfulness (John 15:4-8)
God's armor (Ephesians 6:11-18)
Chastening (Hebrews 12:5-13)
Assurance (2 Timothy 1:12)
Salvation (Matthew 10:22)
Reward (Galatians 6:6-9)

Christians are not only called to believe the gospel, but also to endure whatever challenges they may face because of the gospel. True Christian victory is achieved by enduring different types of sufferings — whether tribulation, distress, persecution, famine, nakedness, peril, or sword — through the love of Christ our Savior.

The story of Job is a familiar one that vividly demonstrates how a believer in God can persevere in the face of extreme hardship and still keep one's faith and integrity intact.

> "My brethren, take the prophets, who spoke in the name of the Lord, as an example of suffering and patience. Indeed we count them blessed who endure. You have heard of the perseverance of Job and seen the end intended by the Lord — that the Lord is very compassionate and merciful" (James 5:10-11).

---

113

Lois Anderson knew this well. Connie and I met Sister Lois when we raised support for our first term as Assemblies of God missionaries to Ecuador. She lived in Epson, Kentucky, and pastored a tiny church. By the time we met her, she'd been ministering in eastern Kentucky for more than 40 years, barely getting by on a shoestring budget. Over spaghetti and ketchup (the only sauce she had in the house) in the back of the church after a Sunday night service, Sister Lois told us how she had built the church with a few volunteers and her own hands. She reminisced how the congregation didn't grow much despite her best efforts, and how finances were always thin. She also explained how, to her amazement, she always managed to find a reason to stay. When I asked why she never left, Sister Lois said she always felt compelled to stay so the community had a place to turn where the gospel could be found.

Sister Lois came to Kentucky in 1951 to help a pastor. When the pastor died, his wife told Sister Lois, "If you stay, I will stay." So, she stayed and worked with this pastor's widow. When the pastor's widow died, Sister Lois decided to move back to her native New York. However, the night before she planned to leave, she had a dream in which the church light was extinguished. She took that to mean that if she left, the church would not continue. So she committed to staying, and she stayed for years.

Lois Anderson was born on June 3, 1928, in Elmira, New York. She attended Zion Bible Institute in East Providence, Rhode Island, and graduated in 1951. She applied for Kentucky Mountain Missions at the age of 23, became a licensed minister in 1959, and was ordained in 1961. In 2011, the Assemblies of God recognized her for 50 years as an ordained minister. She served as the pastor of Tim Branch Missions, Epson, Kentucky, and Faith Assembly of God in Hager, Kentucky, until 1992.

Sister Lois, like Colonel Sanders, had that rare combination of sacrifice, persistence, and patience that makes determination and staying power so effective.

But, you might ask, what's the reward for going if it means life in the backwoods where you're overlooked, often ignored, and barely able to get by on spaghetti noodles and ketchup? I think for us who firmly believe in eternity the answer is clear, "Being strengthened with all power according to His glorious might, so that you may have great endurance and patience, and giving joyful thanks to the Father, who has qualified you to share in the inheritance of His holy people in the kingdom of light" (Colossians 1:11,12).

Yes, this life is temporal. That's okay. Eternity is forever. That's awesome! Go and make as many disciples as you can, so that they, too, can enjoy the eternal rewards that are forthcoming. My son-in-law, Joil Marbut, often says, "Ten percent of missions is showing up; 90 percent is staying." Jesus put it this way: "Don't move around from home to home. Stay in one place, eating and drinking what they provide. Don't hesitate to accept hospitality" (Luke 10:7, NLT).

Back to Sister Lois. Sometime after her death in 2014, we visited a supporting church in Lexington, Kentucky. After the meeting, a well-dressed businessman made his way to thank me for the message I preached. I soon learned that he was a successful lawyer in the city. During the brief conversation, I asked how he had come to faith in Christ. His answer took me back to the spaghetti ketchup dinner in the eastern mountains of Kentucky. As a young child, the successful lawyer found Christ through the loving and caring ministry of Sister Lois Anderson, which led him down the road of higher education.

# S.T.O.P.

**Consider the key word <u>Sandals</u> again and ask yourself the following questions:**

What was Jesus conveying when He said, "Take no <u>sandals</u>"?

What does Jesus want us to understand?

What does this idea mean to me now?

What does Jesus want to convey to me through this command?

**Now let's live it out. How will you respond to what you have heard, read, learned, or felt inspired to do?**

S. SPECIFIC: What specifically will you do in response to the key word <u>Sandals</u>?

T. TIME-SENSITIVE: Within what time frame will you begin or complete the task?

O. OBTAINABLE: Is it possible? If not, go back to S.

P. PERTINENT: How does this goal relate to the key word and our understanding of it?

*Read It - Think It - Write It - Share It*

———

# 8

## Word Eight – Greet
### *Disastrous Distractions*

Key word:  Greet – To salute one, greet, bid welcome, wish well.[97]

Key verse: "...do not greet anyone on the road" (Luke 10:4).

Key Thought: The best of plans, initiatives, and inspiration will fall under the weight of unchecked distractions.

———————

I sat down with a group of new followers of Christ and led them inductively through Luke chapter 10. After we read through the text a couple of times, I asked, "Does something from these words of Jesus grab anyone's attention?" Within seconds, a man in his twenties responded, "Yeah, what's this about not greeting anyone?" I thought, *you have got to be kidding! With all this rich text, he is drawn to, "Do not greet anyone on the road."* Before I could wrap my head around these seemingly misplaced words of Jesus, the young man asked again, "What does that mean, anyway?"

To be honest, after a degree in theology and 40-plus years of pastoring, I didn't have an answer. My theology degree didn't help one bit, but my Master's in Leadership quickly responded, "What do you think it means?"

———————————————

[97] Greek Lexicon. G782 (KJV), *Blue Letter Bible.*

"Well, I think I know what it means," he continued. "It means do not get distracted." I replied, "You are absolutely right, that is a perfect answer!" I hoped no one would pick up on my deer in the headlights moment. Later I went back to see if indeed I had confirmed the correct answer, and sure enough, the response fit. The young new convert hit it dead on the money.

## Curtain of Distraction

Basketball teams playing against the Arizona State University Sun Devils at Fargo Arena struggle at the free throw line because of the "Curtain of Distraction." It's a simple PVC structure with black curtains hanging from it. But just before an opposing player shoots a free throw, the curtains are pulled back to reveal any number of colorful — and extremely distracting — characters, such as dancing unicorns, Elvis impersonators, heavyset men doing aerobics, or creepy clowns. On average, the Curtain of Distraction pushes the converted free throw percentage of opposing teams down nearly 20 percent. That's worth about 2 points per game to the Sun Devils. For many teams in Division I basketball, the margin of victory is less than 2 points per game.

Jesus took a stand against distractions, even seemingly small ones. He knew they could take His followers off course as they went into the world sharing His message of love, grace, and making disciples.

But not stopping to greet anyone seems a little extreme, doesn't it? After all, aren't being friendly, likable, and willing to say hello hallmarks of someone who is so full of Jesus' love that their joy needle can't help but jump off the charts?

When Connie and I embarked on our first missionary term in Ecuador, we plastered genuine smiles on our faces as we left the States. We greeted every driver, ticket agent, flight attendant, stranger, server, pilot, and passenger we came across. We were purveyors of grips and grins.

Looking back now, I can't imagine what I would have thought if Jesus told me explicitly not to greet anyone as we went to the mission field. But when I think of all the people who have slipped into eternity without knowledge of Jesus Christ in the past year, I can't help but think that though the Lord's instructions not to greet anyone may seem rude, they are incredibly on point.

## Napoleon

History is full of stories of people who missed the mark because they became distracted. Every time we sing the "Star Spangled Banner," we commemorate a U.S. battle during the War of 1812. But another famous War of 1812 — the French invasion of Russia — also occurred. (Historians, please forgive me for trying to reduce this complex engagement into a 3-minute teaching tool. However, a portion of the story highlights a human weakness that plagues most all of us.)

In June 1812, Napoleon invaded Russia with perhaps as many as 650,000 soldiers — quite possibly the largest and most diverse European armed force ever assembled up to that point.[98] As they marched on Russia, the Russian army offered little resistance against the French. For more than three months, they retreated toward Moscow with Napoleon's army in hot pursuit.

---

[98] Greenspan, Jesse, "Napoleon's Disastrous Invasion of Russia, 200 Years Ago," History Channel, June 22, 2012, http://www.history.com/news/napoleons-disastrous-invasion-of-russia-200-years-ago.

When the French reached Moscow, a surprised Napoleon found much of the city deserted. But his first night there, Russians who had remained in the city set it on fire. Napoleon waited a month for a fight or a surrender, but neither came. So, on Oct. 18, 1812, he had no choice but to retreat to Paris. Despite the great fire, much wealth remained in the cellars of burnt down houses.[99] Like any good conqueror, he made sure to loot the city as proof of victory.[100]

As his army struggled back to France, one great error of Napoleon's became evident. He allowed his troops to be loaded down with booty as confirmation of their victory. These distractions slowed the army's retreat and made them susceptible to attack. And the Russians did attack. In short order, the Russians decimated what had been the largest army ever assembled. Only 30,000 of Napoleon's soldiers made it home.[101]

Diversions can take a toll on the Church and our personal lives. One of the biggest challenges we must be wary of is the collective power of seemingly small, insignificant, and innocuous distractions.

How often are we distracted by the little rubs of life? How often do the pressures of living up to unrealistic expectations trump reaching into our communities with the love of Jesus? How often do our political dogmas distract from our message

---

[99] Bennett, Lynch, "The Grand Failure: How Logistics of Supply Defeated Napoleon in 1812," *Primary Source: The Indiana University Undergraduate Journal of History*,
http://www.indiana.edu/~psource/PDF/Archive%20Articles/Spring201 1/LynchBennettArticle.pdf.
[100] Smitha, Frank E., "Napoleon's Mistakes in 1808-12," Macrohistory: World History, http://www.fsmitha.com/h3/h34-np4d.html.
[101] Ibid.

of love and grace? How often are we more concerned with telling others what we're against than what we support?

## Suggestions

Motivated from my own experience, I have repeatedly warned pastors and churchgoers about being sidelined by the distractions in life. I've learned to become proactive in setting up boundaries to protect me from this deadly pitfall. Some suggestions follow.

**Remember Chapter 1, <u>Appointed</u>, and our emphasis *focus*.** Don't lose sight of the macro goal. Regardless of hurt feelings or offenses, the Church must be true to its purpose to bring glory to God through making disciples. Once the church is in order and everything is aligned with the same vision and discipleship strategy, the leadership must focus on keeping it that way and say no to anything that tries to get the church out of alignment. This kind of laser beam focus is evident in all the great leaders of the Bible. Jesus didn't let His disciple Peter deter Him from going to the Cross. Jesus stayed focused on His vision. The apostle Paul wasn't afraid to go to Jerusalem, even though other Christ followers tried to convince him to stay away because they feared for his safety.

The same is true for countless other examples in the Bible, including Abraham, Joseph, David, and Jeremiah. They knew how to say no to the distractions and stay focused on the task at hand. We must do likewise if we desire to stay single-minded.

Apple Inc. hasn't started making pizzas for a good reason. The company chose only to sell a few goods and focusing on those changed the world. Therefore, before adding anything new to the church, or to our lives, we should always ask, "Does the new idea align with our strategy, or does it take focus away from it?"

**Make honest and regular evaluations of your vision, mission, goals, strategies, and measurables.** Struggling through the process of writing a vision and mission statement is a powerful exercise. But as we walk through the process, we should seriously consider that the Lord himself spoke to the issue of vision (who we are) and mission (what we do). The vision the Lord has for His creation is that God would be glorified. As we discussed in chapter one, the apostle Paul writes concerning the vision of God, "So whether you eat or drink or whatever you do, do it all for the glory of God." The Old Testament also clarifies the Lord's vision: "Everyone who is called by my name, whom I created for My glory, whom I formed and made."[102] A confrontational Old Testament text is Isaiah 48:9–11, which also clarifies the vision of God for His creation:

> "For My name's sake, I defer My anger; for the sake of My praise I restrain it for you, that I may not cut you off. Behold, I have refined you, but not as silver; I have tried you in the furnace of affliction. For My own sake, for My own sake, I do it, for how should My name be profaned? My glory I will not give to another."

Or as author John Piper puts it concerning the vision of God, "Man was created from the beginning in God's image that he might image forth God's glory."[103]

---

[102] Isaiah 43:7.
[103] Piper, John, "God Created Us for His Glory," 1980. https://www.desiringgod.org/messages/god-created-us-for-his-glory

The Church's mission of bringing God glory is to make disciples. We are not called to build the Church. Jesus said He would do that. We are not even called to be Christian; others label us that. We are called to be and to make disciples.

So, our vision is "to bring glory to God" (or something that conveys that idea) and our mission (the process) is to be and to make disciples of Christ (or something like that). With these ideas in mind, ask the difficult questions. Is everything I am doing revolving around this mission and vision?

**Stop measuring yourself by yourself.** Great wisdom is found in 2 Corinthians 10:12: "We do not dare to classify or compare ourselves with some who commend themselves. When they measure themselves by themselves and compare themselves with themselves, they are not wise."

*How many are you running in attendance? How big is your church?* It's the game we play constantly. The world calls it keeping up with the Joneses. In the church, I call it, "keeping up with the Baptists!"

Whenever we emphasize numbers, we are always disappointed. The figures never will be high enough. God is in charge of the numbers. We are in charge of what He has put us in charge of — but it's not the numbers. We must be careful to concentrate on making disciples, and the numbers will take care of themselves.

There always will be a bigger ministry. Someone always will post a better tweet, write a better book or blog post, or preach a better sermon. When we begin to compare, it distracts us from the ministry we've been God-appointed to lead.[104]

---

[104] Edmondson, Ron. http://churchleaders.com/pastors/pastor-articles/176477-ron-edmondson-dangerous-distractions-for-a-pastor.html

**Get a big case of, as a Florida friend says, "Ion't care"** ("I don't care" Southern style). Say no to anything that tries to get the you or the church out of alignment.

**Dump the luggage.** Are we just looking for any new program, plan, or strategy to add to our already overburdened lives and church agendas? What if we took an honest look at everything we do and began to remove what isn't essential, and, in some instances, what isn't even biblical?

### King Amaziah's Distraction

The story of Amaziah the distracted King is found in 2 Chronicles 25:1-28. He lacked single-mindedness in his obedience to God. Consequently, his life was filled with interferences that led to a disobedient and a defeated walk with God.[105] A divided heart is a distracted heart. At least four things robbed him of his focus:

> Distracted by wanting to do things his way (verses 6-8)
> Distracted by greed (verses 8, 9)
> Distracted by misguided advisers (verses 14-16)
> Distracted by his arrogance (verses 18, 19)

Most of King Amaziah's distractions came internally, not externally. Interestingly, 62 percent of auto accidents come from diversions inside the vehicle, while distractions from outside the vehicle account for 35 percent.[103]

Legendary Dallas Cowboys football coach Tom Landry remarked, "I learned early in sports that to be effective — for a player to play the best he can play — is a matter of

---

[105] UCG. https://www.ucg.org/beyond-today/spiritual-distractions

concentration and being unaware of distractions, positive or negative." [106]

Next, let's talk about getting through some doors, Chapter Nine.

[106] Landry, Tom. https://www.brainyquote.com/authors/tom_landry

# S.T.O.P.

**Consider again the word <u>Greet</u> and the phrase, "Do not greet anyone."**

What was the message that Jesus was conveying to His disciples?

What did Jesus want them to understand?

What does this phrase now mean to me?

What does Jesus want to convey to me through this phrase?

**Now let's live it out. How will you respond to what you have heard, read, learned, or felt inspired to do?**

S. SPECIFIC: What specifically will you do in response to the key phrase, do not <u>greet</u>?

T. TIME-SENSITIVE: Within what time frame will you begin or complete the task?

O. OBTAINABLE: Is it possible? If not, go back to S.

P. PERTINENT: How does this goal relate to the key word and our understanding of it?

*Read It - Think It - Write It - Share It*

# PART FOUR
## *Leap the Leaps*

Words nine, ten and eleven:  Enter - Peace - Eat

We have now come to the place in the *journey* where we are taking huge strides. When one is invited to enter, and then to eat, you are most definitely on your way to building lasting relationships for eternity's sake. Please understand, Jesus is not talking about manipulating and exploiting acquaintances to build an organization. He is teaching His disciples how to establish intentional and profound relationships that produce lasting and eternal rewards.

### Leap the Leaps

Twelve from the drylands of Faran
Returned from exploring the glorious foreign,
Great leaders of the Israelite,
Men of great might.

They gave their report showing much fruit.
"We should be more than able to conquer it.
Milk and honey in the land.
Let's take possession by our hand."

"We can't attack. They're too strong for us."
"Yet, be strong and very courageous."
"We felt as small next to them."
"How we looked ever so thin."

Then you will be prosperous and successful.
Your God will be with you wherever you go.
Be strong and very courageous.
Be sure you will see the miraculous.

"And wherever You send us we will go."
Only be strong, courageous and never say no.
"Whatever you have commanded us, we will do.
May our leaps come into submission only to You."

—W.E.M.

# 9

## Word Nine – Enter
### *Daunting Doors*

Key word: Enter – To go or come into.[107]

Key verse: "When you enter a house …" (Luke 10:5).

Key thought: It's one thing to arrive at a destination, it's quite another to be personally invited to enter into one's place of security and comfort.

---

In 1989, I was ready to take on the world for Jesus. Connie and I recently had moved to Cuenca, and I could not shake an ambitious plan to plant churches in every community in the Ecuadorian province. What I didn't know then — but know now — is that success *and failure* would be the realities of our ministry, whether I liked it or not.

When we first arrived in Cuenca, I looked forward to going to the market each week. With two local friends, we ventured into a rural Andean open market. Though I spoke Spanish, still poorly, my blue eyes and dirty blond hair screamed "tourist." The craftsmen, hawkers, sellers, and shopkeepers equated white skin with dollar signs.

---

[107] Oxford Dictionaries.

*"Mee-ster,"* they would call, trying to garner my attention. "Mister, where are you from?"

"Kentucky," I'd reply. "The United States, Kentucky."

*"Daniel Boone! Do you know Daniel Boone?"* Many of them would ask. How in the world did they know about Kentucky and Daniel Boone in a remote village in the top of the Andes Mountains? I soon learned that the 1960s-television series Daniel Boone had been translated into Spanish and reached the small village through one weak channel from a distant city. (Interestingly, we carry that same series on Unsión TV today.[108])

I'd smile and nod as my new acquaintances peppered me with questions about log cabins, mountains, bears, and guns.

I'd ask, "Do you know Daniel Boone lived 200 years ago? Most of us don't live in log cabins anymore."

*"How can that be?"* they asked incredulously. *"I just saw him on television this week."* (I guess it was then that I learned the power of television and how it can aid in advancing the cause of Christ. Adobe or grass huts may not have a solid floor or running water, but if there is electricity and a television signal, ever how weak, they *will have* a TV!)

As the weeks passed, the conversations grew deeper and more meaningful. I made some genuine connections, and as the transactional relationships in the market moved from exchanging small talk and money for products, true friendships began to form.

"Bill, what are you doing here in Cuenca?" they'd ask.

---

[108] *www.unsion.tv*

"I have come to give a hand when people are in need of hope, or are looking for answers," I'd reply. "Are you a doctor, Bill?"

"No, but I do know how to help someone find peace and hope."

"I'd like you to meet my family. Can you visit my family and me, Bill?"

*"Absolutely!"*

Those invitations to <u>enter</u> into their lives meant everything to me. Though I desperately wanted to share my faith and plant churches, I knew building true friendships that would last the test of time were paramount to any preconceived goals I had. Today, every time I visit that community, I receive hugs, kisses of greeting, and firm handshakes. I also visit the churches born out of those friendships. I'm convinced that many of the congregations we've had the honor of helping plant in Ecuador wouldn't have come into existence if not founded on true friendships that led to invitations to <u>enter</u> into the lives, worlds, and cultures of people who once only viewed me as nothing more than a tourist from whom to extract money.

No wonder the reciprocal pronoun "one another" stands out in the New Testament. This term highlights the importance of belonging to a group that shares life: Outdo one another in showing honor (Romans 12:10). Live in harmony with one another (Romans 12:16). Admonish one another (Romans 15:14). Greet one another with a holy kiss (Romans 16:16). Wait for one another (1 Corinthians 11:33). Have the same care for one another (1 Corinthians 12:25). Be servants of one another (Galatians 5:13). Bear one another's burdens (Galatians 6:2). Comfort one another (1 Thessalonians 5:11). Build one another up (1 Thessalonians 5:11). Be at peace with one another (1 Thessalonians 5:13). Do good to one another (1 Thessalonians 5:15). Put up with one another in love (Ephesians 4:2). Be kind and compassionate to one another (Ephesians 4:32). Submit to one another (Ephesians 5:21). Forgive one another (Colossians 3:13). Confess your sins to one another (James 5:16). Pray for one another (James 5:16). Love one another from the heart (1 Peter 1:22). Be hospitable to one another (1 Peter 4:9).


## Oops!

Like any person with an entrepreneurial spirit, I took note of how others ventured into difficult-to-reach communities. I determined I'd have no trouble adopting — maybe even capitalizing — on their strategies and applying them to the Ecuadorian communities I was bent on reaching them for Jesus. Oops, turns out I was wrong!

The strategy of making true friends, who may or may not invite me to <u>enter</u> their worlds and may or may not ask me to share my faith, which may or may not lead to the planting of a church, takes time. In fact, it often takes a lot of time.

The moment I moved from developing genuine, long-lasting friendships to an in-your-face, urban style, microwave evangelism mode, I became completely ineffective. What had worked for missionary colleagues in the inner city was not going to work in the rural communities of the Andes Mountains.

I learned this one day in a Quichua community, as I stood preaching in an open-air meeting, a man approached me and punched me in the face. "We don't worship your God here." he spat. "*Leave us!*"

I would like to think I suffered persecution for my faith, but in reality, I had been reminded of the fact that I was an unwanted guest, uninvited to <u>enter</u> the man's community. To this day, even after multiple attempts, no church exists there. Even now, when I visit that community, no one welcomes me, no one calls me friend, and no one cares if I stay or leave.

The apostle Paul definitely stirred some opposition in some of the places he preached. However, he didn't merely encounter the ideas and institutions of the people living there; he adopted a deliberate policy of accommodation to them. This comes out most clearly in his first letter to the Christians at Corinth. "I have become all things to all men," he says, "that I might by all means save some" (1 Corinthians 9:22, RSV).[109] He most definitely had moved beyond the threshold of their hearts and dwellings.

Spiritual conversion can take place in an instant, yet transformation usually takes place over time and almost always involves moving through doors of people's homes and hearts. While we still inhabit earth, our transformation will happen by degrees, teaches the apostle,[110] and that usually takes place in direct, beyond the door, relationships of faith.[111]

In every person, there is a longing for true righteousness, love, and unity. Our doors, therefore, should be open to everyone, yet most people are still not ready for community. Consequently, there is not much gained by going out on the streets to call everyone to community.

---

[109] Banks, Robert J. (1994-02-01). *Paul's Idea of Community: The Early House Churches in Their Cultural Setting*, Revised edition (Kindle locations 270-272). Baker Book Group.
[110] 2 Corinthians 3:18.
[111] 1 Corinthians 12.

Many people simply would not be in the position to understand such a call. "They would not be matured enough in their inner development to follow it. God must call them first. The Spirit must speak the living Word into their hearts. Because faith is not given to everybody at the same time, we must wait for the hour which God gives," writes Eberha Arnold.[112]

When someone invites us to <u>enter</u> their world, it's more than a sign; it's an honor that indicates the way is open. We may be permitted to breach their thoughts, their families, and even their faiths. Be warned: When we accept the invitation to <u>enter</u>, we <u>enter</u> into a host of challenges and possibilities.

Jesus said, "When you <u>enter</u> a house, first say, 'Peace to this house.' If someone who promotes peace is there, your peace will rest on them; if not, it will return to you. Stay there, eating and drinking whatever they give you" (Luke 10:5-7). Certainly Jesus believed that church should happen wherever life happens. One shouldn't have to leave life to go to church.[113]

## What Does the Bible Say About Moving Beyond Doors?

"I know all the things you do, and I have opened a door for you that no one can close. You have little strength, yet you obeyed my word and did not deny me" (Revelation 3:8).

"And pray for us, too, that God may open a door for our

---

[112] Arnold, Eberhard. *Called to Community: The Life Jesus Wants for His People* (pp. 80-81). Plough Publishing House.
[113] Cole, Neil. *Organic Church: Growing Faith Where Life Happens*. (p. 134) Baker Books.

message, so that we may proclaim the mystery of Christ, for which I am in chains" (Colossians 4:3).

"There is a wide-open door for a great work here, although many oppose me. When Timothy comes, don't intimidate him. He is doing the Lord's work, just as I am" (1 Corinthians 16:9-10).

"I will give him the key to the house of David — the highest position in the royal court. When he opens doors, no one will be able to close them; when he closes doors, no one will be able to open them" (Isaiah 22:22).

"Upon arriving in Antioch, they called the church together and reported everything God had done through them and how he had opened the door of faith to the Gentiles, too" (Acts 14:27).

"When I came to the city of Troas to preach the good news of Christ, the Lord opened a door of opportunity for me"[114] (2 Corinthians 2:12).

## Doors bring unique and cultural challenges

Moving beyond the porch, literally or figuratively, can be quite daunting. The first time I walked into a pastor's fellowship meeting in Cuenca, Ecuador with several local ministers, I knew I would be the only North American in the room.

With only a few more than ten congregations established in Cuenca — a city of 250,000 people — evangelicals like myself represented a tiny minority.

---

[114] Chery, Fritz. *Doors* (2017-02-27) *http://biblereasons.com/doors*

Finding favor with local ministers proved to be crucial to my goal of planting churches in the province.

I arrived about 10 minutes early and failed to realize that such meetings in this culture included sharing a meal.

I politely requested less portions due to the fact that I had just eaten prior to the meeting. After an hour and a half of discussion and then idle conversation, I politely said my goodbyes to a couple of the pastors. On all fronts, I had done everything textbook perfect, according to my American upbringing.

I found out later that I had broken at least four cultural rules that offended my new colleagues: Arriving early, not eating all food prepared for me, leaving the gathering early, and not individually telling everyone goodbye. In the weeks following the meeting, I spent many hours asking for forgiveness and learning cultural norms from my merciful brothers.

Perhaps the reason Jesus places such emphasis on <u>entering</u> and staying is that building true friendships, which can birth true disciples, takes time and requires us to learn some awkward, often embarrassing, lessons. Union in the Spirit involves union with one another, for the Spirit is primarily a shared, not individual, experience. It is something that must be worked at and surely mistakes will be made.

## Using television as an open door

When we launched a television station in Cuenca, we based many of our philosophical strategies for doing business and ministry on the stressful lessons I learned in plant churches.
Doing so compelled us to take an uncommon approach to Christian television. We viewed television as an invitation beyond the thresholds of hearts and homes.

Instead of doing *Christian* television, our main goal focused on *Christians doing* television. After all, can television really be *Christian?* The second element involved airing only programming that brought glory to God.

If it did, we showed programs whether or not people thought they were "Christian" enough.

We had a simple vision: Be disciples of Jesus living out our lives through programing that would honor God and bring Him glory. In place of "religious" news, we just delivered high quality news coverage. We saw our programming as simply a tool of discipleship. Soon after launching, our metrics told us that people watched our programs because we had excellent sports, news, family-oriented teaching, and entertainment programming. As viewers watched, they learned about Christ and His message of hope and love. After years now of persistence, perseverance and patience, the results are more than impressive.

As you may have noticed, we are back to the same theme we talked about under the subject of sandals. Remember? You won't need two pairs of sandals because you won't wear out the first pair. Here again, the idea of staying comes into focus. If the home is deserving, <u>enter</u> and stay. Jesus plainly says, "Don't be moving from house to house."

### Don't Quit
*By William Murray Angus*

*When things go wrong, as they sometimes will,*
*When the road you're trudging seems all uphill,*
*When the funds are low and the debts are high,*
*And you want to smile, but you have to sigh,*
*When care is pressing you down a bit,*
*Rest if you must, but don't you quit.*

---

*Life is strange with its twists and turns,*
*As everyone of us must sometimes learn,*
*And many a failure turns about,*
*When he might have won if he'd stuck it out,*
*Don't give up though the pace seems slow,*
*You may succeed with another blow.*

*Success is failure turned inside out,*
*The silver tint of the clouds of doubt,*
*And you can never tell how close you are,*
*It may be near when it seems afar,*
*So stick to the fight when you're hardest hit,*
*It's when things seem worst that you mustn't quit.*

# S.T.O.P.

**Consider the word <u>Enter</u> again and ask yourself the following questions:**

What was Jesus conveying to His disciples through the idea of <u>Enter</u>?

What did Jesus want them to understand about this idea of <u>Entering</u>?

What does this word <u>Enter</u> now mean to me?

What does Jesus want to convey to me through the word <u>Enter</u>?

**Now let's live it out. How will you respond to what you have heard, read, learned, or felt inspired to do?**

S. SPECIFIC: What specifically will you do in response to the word <u>ENTER</u>?

T. TIME-SENSITIVE: Within what time frame will you begin or complete the task?

O. OBTAINABLE: Is it possible? If not, go back to S.

P. PERTINENT: How does this goal relate to the key word and our understanding of it?

*Read It - Think It - Write It - Share It*

———

# 10

## Word 10 – Peace
### *Likable Links*

Key word:  Peace – Freedom from disturbance; quiet and tranquility.[115]

Key verse: "Peace to this house" (Luke 10:5).

Key thought: People of Peace are individuals with whom you "click" in a wholesome way. Jesus calls His disciples to nurture such connections.

---

I was negotiating a treacherous mountain road late one night. Rain pelted the windshield, and my eyes felt heavy. More than anything, I wanted to pull over and sleep. But I was determined to press through because I wanted to get back to Cuenca, our home. I didn't know at the time that God would use my late-night drive to establish a ministry in a tiny village tucked high in the Andes Mountains. God would teach me a lesson on the importance of not only living a peaceful life, but also about the power of connecting with people of peace.

Cutting through the darkness of night, I looked at the glowing numbers on the dashboard's clock and sighed. Well past two in the morning, I still had at least an hour to drive.

---

[115] Oxford Dictionaries.

As I rounded yet another tight corner, I saw someone walking along the side of the road.

"Did you see that?" I asked my passenger as I braked hard. "Was that a woman?" Perhaps sleep deprivation had made me delirious.

We finally stopped, and I threw the truck into reverse. I rolled down the passenger-side window and leaned across the front seat.

"May I help you, ma'am? Do you need a ride?" "*Yes, sir*" was her response. "I need to go to town." "Hop in; we're headed that way," I replied.

The woman climbed into the truck out of the rain. As she did, she gently swung her wet shawl to the front of her and pulled a baby from beneath the covering. As any mother would do, she looked down on her baby and smiled, knowing the baby girl now would be safe. Yet apprehension remained.

"My baby is sick."
"We will take you to the clinic, then."
*"Thank you, kind sir."*

As we drove, I could sense the young mother's worry. To help ease her fears, I asked about her life. She told me she lived in a small village without electricity, running water, stores, and — most importantly — no doctors or clinics. Thus, her late-night walk.

I knew she had to have walked from some village in the mountains to the trailhead that began at the dirt and gravel road we were traveling.

"How long is the walk from your village to the road?"
*"Four hours."*

As we drove, she told me of the difficulties of living in such a remote place. She didn't complain, yet her words spoke of the harsh realities of life in some Ecuadorian villages. When we reached the clinic, she smiled and thanked us for the ride. I prayed for her and her child, then reached into my pocket and gave her a handful of cash.

"We'd like to visit your village to check on you and your baby. Would that be okay?"

*"Yes, please do. Thank you, sir."*

Three weeks later, I stood at the trailhead of the route we hoped would take us to the young mother's village. I looked at my team, quickly inventoried the supplies we would leave in the village, then offered a prayer before embarking on the hike.

We started at 13,000 feet. The air felt thin and in short supply. Thankfully, the trail descended into a deep valley. Four hours later, having nearly descended a mile into the valleys of the Andes, we arrived at the village.

There, we found adobe homes, a small adobe church that doubled as a school, and nearly 100 smiling residents — including the young mother. Her eyes beamed as she held her healthy baby daughter. Like a seasoned public relations specialist, she led us on a tour of her village and introduced us to everyone who lived there. As she did, our team distributed Bibles and supplies to each family.

After a day visiting and ministering to the young mother and the others in her village, we hiked back to the main road and made plans to return. As happens with so many good intentions, the days turned into weeks, the weeks to months, and the months to years.

On several occasions, I drove past the trailhead and thought of the young mother, her village and my promise to return. Each time I drove past, I prayed that God would send someone back to the village to minister.

Ten years later, a young couple from our home church in the States sensed a call to assist us in Ecuador. Soon after, they joined us in Cuenca, and we decided their first adventure would be a trek to Patul, the young mother's village. While excited to be returning, I felt uneasy because so much time had elapsed since we last visited.

As I contemplated the decade that had passed, I came across Luke 10:5-6: "When you enter a house, first say, 'Peace to this house.' If someone who promotes peace is there, your peace will rest on them; if not, it will return to you." Though I couldn't shake my apprehension, the verse gave me a sense of peace I lacked, and we pressed forward with plans to return to Patul.

As I unwittingly played out one scenario after the other in my head, God reminded me of the Roman centurion Cornelius, "a righteous and God-fearing man ... respected by all the Jewish people."[116]

Cornelius had invited Peter into his home and welcomed the apostle warmly. I wanted the same in Patul, but the fact is, when we are called to go, we never can know for sure how people will treat us.

After all, we are called to go as lambs among wolves. That's part of the adventure. If we can fully trust God, it is one of the greatest parts of the *journey*.

---

[116] Acts 10:22.

Though my mind was anxious, my soul found comfort in Cornelius' response to Peter. The Bible says he made Peter feel welcomed. Not only that, he invited his entire family and friends to come and hear Peter's message of salvation. The result? Many believed and were baptized.

The day we hiked down into Patul for only the second time, I felt happy that we brought gifts. Once again, we had Bibles, supplies, and an expectation that God went before us. I convinced myself before we departed that I shouldn't be anxious about who would welcome us; our peace would either rest on someone or it wouldn't. I couldn't do anything about that. Still, I allowed myself to worry.

Who would be the person of peace I would encounter in Patul? Who would welcome us, the messengers? Who would be receptive to our transmission of peace and love? Who would want to continue to share our message with others?

The young mother and her people were Highland Quichua. I knew from experience of their culture, beliefs, and ways that they yearned for people of peace to visit them. That was the good news. But the bad news was we had let so much time pass between visits I couldn't help but wonder if they'd be as receptive as before.

Plus, part of their vetting process involved guinea pigs that run freely around their homes. The guinea pigs are a tasty delicacy, but also according to their traditions, are able to test the spirit of visitors who enter their dwellings. If their guinea pigs started to squeal, it was a sure sign — according to the Quichua — that a visitor was not a person of peace. Oh, the horror!

Any relational equity we had the first time we visited would be squandered. It might sound silly, but as we hiked, I prayed

145

earnestly that God would lead us to that person of peace[117] rather than allow our fate to be determined by superstition and guinea pigs.

## Being a Person of Peace

If we truly know Jesus, we should be the most peaceful people on earth, right? Jesus says, "Peace I leave with you; my peace I give you. I do not give to you as the world gives. Do not let your hearts be troubled and do not be afraid" (John 14:27). Because Jesus, the Prince of Peace, calms us, we should go boldly into any situation fueled by His peace and assurance that He goes before us.

Does that mean we will be met, everywhere we go, with peace? Absolutely not. But that reality should not rattle us or deter us from going. Instead, if we go somewhere and are not met with peace, we should merely feel prompted to move on to another place, where a person of peace is waiting. Incredibly, people of peace are waiting for us. We just have to go.

If we live and go with peace, it forces us to let God take care of all our worries and concerns. Think of it this way: as you hike to your Patul, either God is in control, or you're in big trouble. But the fact is, God is in control, even if you are in big trouble!

Choose to go in peace, trust God, and allow Him to carry all your burdens. Doing so will allow you to be as effective as you need to be so that the gospel can move forward unfettered by your earthly concerns.

---

[117] More discussion of "People of Peace" is found near the end of this chapter.

"Be still, and know that I am God."[118] Peace is at the heart of the gospel. As followers of Jesus in a divided and violent world, we are committed to finding nonviolent alternatives and learning how to make peace between individuals, within and among churches, in society, and between nations.[119]

> "Here is My servant, whom I uphold, My chosen One in whom I delight; I will put My Spirit on Him, and He will bring justice to the nations. He will not shout or cry out, or raise His voice in the streets. A bruised reed He will not break, and a smoldering wick He will not snuff out. In faithfulness, He will bring forth justice" (Isaiah 42:1-4).

## Good Report

I'm glad to report that when we arrived in Patul, the villages warmly received us. Our team played with the children and chatted with the local elders. One woman, a mother of five children, invited us to her home, where she had prepared a feast. As we ate and fellowshipped, I realized she was the person of peace I sought. "Do you think we could return to your village on a regular basis and help the village with some of their basic needs?" I asked.

"Yes, I've been praying that God would send someone to help my people," was her sincere reply, "and now you're here."

I leaned back and smiled. God indeed had gone before us. He led us to a person of peace. He wanted His church to grow, and the people in a tiny village in the middle of the Andes to know Him.

---

[118] Psalm 46:10.
[119] Murray, Stuart. *The Naked Anabaptist*, (p. 24) Herald Press.

I couldn't help but beam as our team shared a time of peace with a new friend who had been praying for our arrival. Who is praying for your arrival? Where is your presence of peace needed? Are you willing to go so that others might know Him?

## More Details About a Person of Peace

While reading a blog by J.R. Woodward, I ran across two authors that brought more clarity to the subject "person of peace."[120]

Mary Hopkins' book *Evangelism Strategies* is a wealth of strategic and practical applications. I highly recommend it to those who are serious about living out the *journey*. I have taken six principles from her work as a guide to better understand the progression of "a person of peace."[121]

**People** – Where is the harvest ripe? Where do you already see God at work? Where has God called you to a harvest field and given you a promise in your heart that you're going to see a response? Know your mission field; know the people upon whom God has called you to focus.[122]

**Prayer** – Prayer is a key feature of Jesus' instructions for mission. In both the sending of the 12 and the 72, Jesus makes the same appeal: "Ask the Lord of the harvest, therefore, to send out workers into his harvest field" (Matthew 9:38 and Luke 10:2).[123]

---

[120] Woodward, J.R., The Person of Peace. (2013-10) *http://jrwoodward.net/2013/10/the-person-of-peace-and-their-oikos*
[121] Hopkins, Mary. *Evangelism Strategies* (pp. 757-759). Alderway Publishing.
[122] Ibid., pp. 835-838.
[123] Ibid., pp. 821-822.

**Process** – As Jesus sent out His disciples on this evangelistic enterprise, He clearly had a process in mind. He understood that all people are on a *journey* of faith, so time is of the essence. He tells His disciples "the harvest is ripe." [124]

**Place** – This is really important. Jesus did not send His disciples out with a mission strategy of attracting people onto their territory on their terms. He sent His disciples out to look for people who responded to them — who welcomed them — to stay with hosts on their terms. [125]

**Partnership** – It's a matter of "receive what is put before you." We often think that evangelism is about what we give. While sacrificial service is our approach to mission engagement, it should never be the only way. [126]

**Peace** – Jesus instructs that the gospel is communicated only when a relationship has been established. This happens through receiving what is given, sharing words of truth, and living alongside them. The lifestyle of the giver reinforces the words spoken and demonstrates the transformation and power that is promised. [127]

## A Person of Receptivity

Tom Wolf defined a person of peace from Luke 10. "A person of peace is a person of receptivity. He or she is an individual prepared by God to receive the Christ follower and the gospel even before one arrives.

[124] Ibid., pp. 877-879.
[125] Ibid., pp. 1002-1004.
[126] Ibid., pp. 1040-1041.
[127] Ibid., pp. 1066-1067.

When we consider discipleship or evangelism, we usually think of sowing seed as the first step. Interestingly however, Jesus tells His disciples, 'Look, the fields are ready for harvest.' This implies that wherever we may go, or are sent, the Lord of the harvest has people ready to be won. The Lord goes on to say that if you find no person of peace, move on. So, make careful plans and strategies, but hold these lightly in your hand so that the Spirit of God can be your director. As we saw earlier, Cornelius became one such individual."[128]

A person of peace is a person of reputation, good or bad. Remember Mark 5 when Jesus lands at Gadarene and is greeted by a demoniac who is violent, naked, in broken chains, and has a horrible reputation? God had sovereignly placed him there, ready for the gospel. A demoniac is not one we would normally see as a "person of peace," but he became that.

This man, after release and conversion, entreats Jesus to permit him to accompany Him. The townspeople and owners of the swine beg Jesus to leave the area. Jesus sends the former demon-possessed man back to Decapolis to "tell." In Mark 7, Jesus returns to Decapolis and now the same people plead with Jesus to stay and touch their sick and paralyzed. The demoniac's extended family saw a changed man, a godly "man of peace" proclaiming Jesus (even though he probably had only a few minutes of discipling).

A person of peace is a person of referral. Scientists call the lead fish that turns first "the fish of reference." Have you ever seen a fish school accident? There are no collisions or accidents.

---

[128] Wolf, Tom. "Persons of Peace." Golden Gate Theological Seminary *http://www.kncsb.org/resources/PersonsofPeace.pdf.*

The "person of <u>peace</u>" becomes the "fish of reference," and he *turns first* in his group.

Through this *one,* God will "turn" an entire *oikos.*[129]

Take your time and *look* for the person of <u>peace</u>.[130]

I want to challenge you, *as* you walk through your day, to be attentive to the people of <u>peace</u> that the Lord *will* send your way. This is *key* to making the most of the discipleship *journey.*

Next on the *journey,* let's eat!

---

[129] The ancient Greek word *oikos* refers to the basic family unit in Greek culture.
[130] Wolf, Tom. "Persons of Peace." Golden Gate Theological Seminary *http://www.kncsb.org/resources/PersonsofPeace.pdf*

# S.T.O.P.

**Consider the key word again and ask yourself the following questions:**

What was Jesus conveying to His disciples when spoke of <u>Peace</u> in the context of Luke 10?

What did Jesus want them to understand?

What does this word now mean to me?

What does Jesus want to convey to me through this word?

**Now let's live it out. How will you respond to what you have heard, read, learned, or felt inspired to do?**

S. SPECIFIC: What specifically will you do in response to the key word <u>Peace</u>?

T. TIME-SENSITIVE: Within what time frame will you begin or complete the task?

O. OBTAINABLE: Is it possible? If not, go back to S.

P. PERTINENT: How does this goal relate to the key word and our understanding of it?

*Read It - Think It - Write It - Share It*

# 11

## Word Eleven – Eat
### *Meaningful Meals*

Key word: Eat – To take food, eat a meal [131]

Key verse: ...eat what is offered to you." (Luke 10:8)

Key thought:  One of the very best opportunities for discipleship is found during a shared meal.

---

Jesus knows that to share a meal with another requires a minimum level of trust that can lead to deeper relationships, which can be a crucial key to spiritual transformation.

Whether you're called (and we all are) to a foreign or domestic field, the call to go requires you to be in proximity and available to those you are called to reach. If we are not eating with those we hope to disciple, we are missing out on one of eternity's greatest opportunities. The simple invitation of Jesus to His friend is, "Come and have breakfast" (John 21:12).

### Minga

Members of the church had gathered for a workday — or a

---

[131] Greek Lexicon. G2068 (KJV), *Blue Letter Bible.*

*minga* — as the Highland Quichuas call it. Our goal: build a drainage system on an elderly couple's mountainous property. Under the hot sun, yet very light air, we dug into the earth side by side with our shovels. The arduous work made us tired. As the lunch hour drew near, the elderly couple invited the other men and me to a meal.

Inside the elderly couple's humble home, I noticed a thick, black soot on the thatched-palm ceiling. Mismatched wooden chairs sat around a rickety wooden table. Overhead, thick, smoky air hung in the dining room. I spotted little knickknacks here and there. As we sat down, steaming bowls of chicken-foot soup and freshly popped popcorn greeted us. On shiny plates sat thick slices of farm-fresh cheese and huge lima beans. Sweet juice filled jelly-type jars, chipped from years of use. A large loaf of piping-hot bread served as the meal's crowning achievement.

It represented a meal fit for kings. I soon learned that Jesus Christ was the real centerpiece of the meal. Our host, "Don" (Mr.) Quichimbo, sat at the head of the table and made eye contact with each of us. Then he quietly cleared his throat and prayed: "Father, as we break bread together, we renew our covenant with You, remembering Your death and celebrating Your resurrection and soon return."

Mr. Quichimbo took the hot bread in his leathery hands and, with a slight tremor, broke it in two as he thanked God for His provisions, love, and for sending friends to help him and his wife with the drainage ditch. He then prayed a prayer of thanks as he passed the bread. Like a true servant, he turned to his wife and grandchildren and served them before serving himself. After everyone had been served, Mr. Quichimbo prayed again.

"This is Your body given for us. We accept Your sacrifice for our sins through this act of faith."

Each of us took a bite of bread and placed the remaining portion on our plates. Mr. Quichimbo then raised his jelly jar of juice. *"And by Your blood, we're forgiven."* In unison, we drank and said, "Amen."

Throughout the meal, the bread plate kept being refilled, as did the jars of juice. Though Mr. Quichimbo and his family would be considered among the poorest of the poor, they gave generously and sacrificially. It marked one of the most memorable meals of my life.

At times during the meal, I sat back and listened and observed the experiences unfolding around the table. The varied conversations ranged from animated to hushed. I heard stories of God's goodness and narratives from the past woven into hope for the future. It proved to be an amazing experience, like none I had ever encountered. On a spiritual level, I couldn't help but marvel that every bite of bread, spoonful of soup, and drop of juice represented an extension of the Lord's Supper.

Perhaps, I thought, one of the most effective ways to make disciples is to simply gather with them and eat.

I later learned that celebrating the Lord's Supper didn't constitute a one-time deal for Mr. Quichimbo and his family. He took time on a regular basis to acknowledge God's sacrifices and love in front of his family, friends, and even strangers who confessed Jesus as their Savior.

While Mr. Quichimbo didn't work as an official minister, his heart seemed to line up with how Jesus would have done things. His humble house certainly didn't symbolize a liturgical setting in which to partake of Communion. But there were — a handful of followers of Jesus, sitting on handmade wooden chairs, celebrating the Lord's Supper under a thatched roof. I couldn't help but ask myself: Is this what

Jesus intended for His church when He led the Last Supper? In the months following I wondered if we — as the Church — had somehow reduced Communion to nothing more than a monthly religious rite complete with factory-stamped miniature breads and prepackaged plastic cups of juice so that we could get on with our services. I also thought about the power of gathering to eat. It seemed that we, the Church, missed the mark on both experiences, for "Kingdom living is fundamentally social. It involves membership, citizenship, loyalties, and identity."[132]

## Deipnon

The word *deipnon* (1 Corinthians 11:20), meaning "dinner," tells us that Communion didn't symbolize a token meal (as it has become since) or part of a meal (as it is sometimes envisaged), but rather an entire, ordinary meal. The term indicates that this is the main (normally evening) meal, the one to which guests were invited.[133]

Its character as an ordinary meal is retained even though it has been given new significance. Paul's injunctions to the "hungry" to eat before they leave home (verses 22, 34) do not represent the beginnings of a separation of the Lord's Supper from the meal itself. He is merely trying to avoid abuses that had entered into the meal at Corinth. Nowhere does Paul suggest that the Lord's Supper has any cultic significance. With the exception of the words that accompany it, the meal didn't differ from the customary one for guests in a Jewish home. The breaking and distribution of the bread typified the

---

[132] Kraybill, Donald B. (2012-11-21). *The Upside-Down Kingdom* (pp. 202). Herald Press.

[133] Spirit of the Master. *https://spiritofthemaster.blogspot.com/2015/08/why-do-people-eat-lords-supper-in_17.html*

normal way of commencing such a meal, just as the taking of a cup was the usual way to bring it to a conclusion. Prayers of blessing accompanied both.[134]

I decided to dive into the New Testament and study how Jesus and His disciples ate. As I did, I realized amazing, deep, and bonding times of fellowship occurred not just during Communion. In fact, Jesus and His disciples regularly used times of eating to reflect, commune, share, inspire, and grow closer to one another and to God.

> "Breaking bread from house to house, they ate their food with gladness and simplicity of heart, praising God and having favor with all the people. And the Lord added to the church daily those who were being saved."[135]

F.F. Bruce in his book *Acts of the Apostles* says the fellowship spoken of in Acts 2 was "the breaking of bread." This represented "something more than the ordinary partaking of food together: the regular observance of the Lord's Supper is no doubt indicated ... this observance appears to have formed the part of an ordinary meal."[136]

About the Early Church, Robert Banks wrote, "The most general form of meeting, however, centered around the eating of a meal and the exercise of ministry for each other's benefit."[137]

---

[134] Banks, Robert J. *Paul's Idea of Community: The Early House Churches in Their Cultural Setting*, revised edition (Kindle locations 1570-1578). Baker Book Group.

[135] Acts 2:46,47, NKJV.

[136] Bruce, F.F. *Acts of the Apostles* (p. 79) Wm. B. Eerdmans Publishing Co.

[137] Banks, Robert J., *Paul's Idea of Community: The Early House Churches in Their Cultural Setting*, (Kindle locations 1570-1578). Baker Book Group.

---

"Sharing tables is one of the most uniquely human things we do," writes Barry Jones. "No other creature consumes its food at a table. And sharing tables with other people reminds us that there's more to food than fuel. We don't <u>eat</u> only for sustenance."[138] I ran across the ministry of Barry Jones while attending an Alpha Course taught by Nicky Gumble at Irving Bible Church in Texas. His article "The Dinner Table as a Place of Connection, Brokenness, and Blessing" enlightened me.

Jones suggests that the dinner table is a place where connection, blessing, brokenness, and forgiveness can and should be taking place. His observations follow.

## The Table as a Place of Connection

Tables are one of the most important places of human connection. New Testament scholar N. T. Wright captured this sentiment when he wrote, "When Jesus himself wanted to explain to His disciples what His forthcoming death was all about, He didn't give them a theory, He gave them a meal."

I'm convinced that one of the most important spiritual disciplines for us to recover in the kind of world in which we live is the discipline of table fellowship. In the fast-paced, tech-saturated, attention-deficit-disordered culture in which we find ourselves, Christians need to recover the art of a slow meal around a table with people we care about. "Table fellowship" often doesn't make the list of the classical spiritual disciplines.

---

[138] Park, Melonie. *"The Dinner Table, A Place of Brokenness and Blessing"*.
http://meloniepark.org/article/the-dinner-table-as-place-of-connection-brokenness-and-blessing

But in the midst of a world that increasingly seems to have lost its way with regard to matters of both food and the soul, Christian spirituality has something important to say about the way that sharing tables nourishes us both physically and spiritually. We need a recovery of the spiritual significance of *what we eat*, *where we eat*, and *with whom we eat*.

## The Table as a Place of Blessing

The table is a place to remember the blessing of God. One ancient prayer of the Church (based on an even more ancient Hebrew prayer) says, "Blessed are you, O Lord God, King of the Universe, for you give us food to sustain our lives and make our hearts glad." We need to recover the importance of gathering with people around our tables for the purpose of enjoying a meal as both a gift and means of grace. These meals are what the Celts called "thin places" —where the veil that separates heaven and earth seems exceedingly thin.

## The Table as a Place of Brokenness

One of my favorite meal scenes in all of Scripture occurs on the banks of the Sea of Galilee after the resurrection of Jesus. It's recorded in **John 21**. After a futile night of fishing, the disciples encounter Jesus, who calls out to them from the shore. Acting impulsively, as always, Peter dives into the water fully clothed in an effort to reach Jesus. As he emerges from the sea, dripping wet, he moves toward Jesus, who has made a fire on the beach. And at that moment he discerns a hauntingly familiar smell. The word that John the storyteller uses to describe the fire that Jesus made is a word that occurs in only one other place in Scripture — earlier in his own story (**John 18:18**).

There the word describes the fire where Peter and the others warmed themselves on the night of Jesus's arrest and trial. The charcoal fire of **John 18:18** was the place of Peter's denial. For Peter, shame had a smell — that of burning charcoal. But the charcoal fire of **John 21** is the place of Peter's restoration. The simple invitation of Jesus to His friend is, "Come and have breakfast" (21:12).

The table is the place where broken sinners find connection and belonging. Despite our best intentions, we all, like Peter, stumble after Jesus. We desperately need people who will *journey* with us in our stumbling. We need to recover table fellowship as a spiritual discipline in order to strengthen the bonds of spiritual friendship among believers who are walking together on the road of discipleship.

## The Table as a Place of Forgiveness

I'm convinced that our dinner tables have the potential to be the most "missional" places in all of our lives. Perhaps before we invite people to Jesus or even invite them to church, we should invite them to dinner.

If table fellowship is a spiritual discipline that is vital for shaping and sustaining our life with God for the world, we need to make a point to share our tables with people who are in our lives, but far from God. This was one of the most distinctive aspects of Jesus's ministry.

## Every Table an Altar

Yehiel E. Poupko, a Jewish rabbi, pointed to the crucial need of seeing the table as the family altar. The priestly blessing is now recited over children by parents, who take the place of priests in the temple. Thus, can we now say, "Every home a temple; every family a sanctuary; every table an altar; every meal an offering; every Jew a Priest."

Intimate activities that people do together include loving, playing, praying, working, and eating. Animals feed; humans eat. Eating, for humans, is a social task which transforms the biological need into a community of intimacy and shared experience. People sit around a table or some other shared space. They face each other. Someone has prepared the food, someone serves the food, and people pass food to each other.

Jewish tradition recognizes a meal as a time for intimacy, fellowship, and significant conversation. Kindness is the basic mood of the Jewish meal. People are fed and nourished, and in this intimate setting people talk with each other about what matters. That is why the rabbis say that if people eat together and Torah talk is not exchanged, then the meal is a vain enterprise. If eating does not create the opportunity to teach and to learn, then it becomes merely biological feeding.[139]

## Back to Mr. Quichimbo's Table

As I discovered at the Quichimbos' family table, heartfelt meals centered on Jesus Christ create uncommon moments of communion that are transformative for believers and unbelievers. When I use communion with a lowercase 'c,' I am not referring to Communion, the Lord's Supper. To break bread with a non-Christian is not what I am advocating, as that would go against the Lord's instruction. I am suggesting that meals are perfect times to commune with others — including those without faith — so that all can hear, feel, and see Christ's love and grace through our actions, ideas, and words.

---

[139] Poupko, Rabbi Yehiel E., "*Eating as a Celebration of Jewish Life*," *JUF News*.

161

From what I've read in the Bible and experienced in situations like the one around the Quichimbos' table, one of the most authentic places for honest conversation, transparency, deep worship, and effective evangelism can be found around tables where meals are shared. Perhaps there we can strengthen our faith with other followers of Jesus and share our hope with those in need of a Savior.

No wonder Jesus added "<u>eat</u>" to the discipleship *journey*. Are we <u>eating</u> together to make disciples, or just with our church friends? Have our local churches missed the mark by abbreviating the Communion celebration?

"Every home a temple; every family a sanctuary; every table an altar; every meal an offering; every [believer] a priest."[140]

---

[140] Ibid.

# S.T.O.P.

**Consider the key word <u>Eat</u> again and ask yourself the following questions:**

What was Jesus conveying to His disciples?

What did Jesus want them to understand when he tells them to <u>Eat</u>?

What does this word now mean to me?

What does Jesus what to convey to me through the word <u>Eat</u>?

**Now let's live it out. How will you respond to what you have heard, read, learned, or felt inspired to do?**

S. SPECIFIC: What specifically will you do in response to the key word?

T. TIME-SENSITIVE: Within what time frame will you begin or complete the task?

O. OBTAINABLE: Is it possible? If not, go back to S.

P. PERTINENT: How does this goal relate to the key word and our understanding of it?

*Read It - Think It - Write It – Share It*

# PART FIVE
*Enjoy the Joy*

Key words twelve and thirteen: Heal – Tell

Living out the *journey* as a disciple of Christ can come with great sacrifices and burdens, for "pain and suffering are always inevitable for a large intelligence and a deep heart. The really great men *and women* must, I think, have great sadness on earth."[141] But as the psalmist writes, "Weeping may stay for the night, but rejoicing comes in the morning."[142] And this is true for disciple makers as well, when in the opportunities to heal and tell we will surely find great joy. And when it comes, enjoy the joy!

## Joy

At the next curve or mountainous hill
Surely there we will find our fill
and yet we push on, never enough
never satisfied, never giving up
looking for joy in very strange places
finally finding it in lost faces.
—W.E.M.

---

[141] Dostoevsky, Fyodor. *Crime and Punishment* (p. 195). Waxkeep Publishing.
[142] Psalm 30:5.

---

# 12

## Word Twelve – <u>Heal</u>
### *Therapeutic Theology*

Key word: <u>Heal</u> – To cure, restore to health[143]

Key verse: "<u>Heal</u> the sick who are there…" (Luke 10:9).

Key thought: All people hurt, struggle, suffer or are wounded, everyone! We all need <u>healing</u>, and Jesus call us to do just that, <u>heal</u>.

————————

At 21 years of age, I began to struggle with a mild depression upon waking up in the morning. It dissipated as my day got underway. Regrettably, the older I got, the more I struggled with morning depression. This left me feeling nearly hopeless, a horrible way to start the day even though the depression would lift after breakfast and a shower.

My depression made no sense. I couldn't fathom anyone understanding what I went through. This fueled a deeper sense of anxiety, which compounded the situation.

I read all I could find on the subject, and I spoke with Christian counselors. Despite my best efforts, I experienced

————————

[143] Greek Lexicon. G2323 (KJV), *Blue Letter Bible.*

————

very little relief, but by God's grace I was able to fulfill my obligations and enjoy life, though living it with an emotional limp.

More than anything I wanted to be <u>healed</u>, but I had not come to the point of needing, or at least being willing to seek professional help. After all, I had made a commitment to follow Jesus years before. Surely the Lord could and would <u>heal</u> me when He wanted.

Looking back now, the Lord already had sent His <u>healers</u>. I just wouldn't turn to them for help.

It's like the story of a man stranded on a deserted island who prayed for the Lord to save him. On three occasions, boats came by and tried to help the castaway. In each case, the lost soul responded to the offer of help saying, "No worry, the Lord will rescue me."

God's <u>healing</u> touch can come divinely or through medicine. It can come immediately, or it can come over a lengthy stretch of time. The point is we just need to be open to however and whenever God wants to <u>heal</u> us.

## Suffering

Throughout the world, people are suffering. About half of adults will experience some sort of cancer.[144] A recent AARP study found 35 percent of adults age 45 and older feel lonely.[145]

---

[144] Crain, Esther, "*New Study: 1 in 2 People Will Get Cancer,*" *Men's Health,* April 1, 2015.
[145] Anderson, Gretchen, "Loneliness Among Older Adults: A National Survey of Adults 45+," *AARP,* September 2010.

Hundreds of thousands of people will suffer from the flu on any given day. More than 20 million Americans are addicted to alcohol or drugs.[146] Half of college students struggle with suicidal thoughts.[147] Nearly 28 percent of children in developing countries are underweight or stunted, and one out every two children lives in poverty.[148]

We live on a planet filled with hurting and sick people. An even more troublesome reality is so many of us are great at hiding our needs or are not willing to seek help, either from God or from those whom He has gifted in medicine.

### Earning the Right to be Heard

Isn't it interesting that this discipleship process, as presented by Jesus in Luke 10:1-9, deals almost entirely with reaching the hearer and earning the right to be heard? Once we earn those rights, then Jesus calls His disciples to <u>heal</u>, then tell.

Let's not skip over this important point: The discipleship *journey* deals mostly with getting to the hearer and earning the right to be heard. But after earning the right to be heard, the first ministry is to <u>heal</u>. And as we have already noted, everyone needs <u>healing</u>.

### Therapy

The Greek word used in Luke 10:9 for *heal* is *therapeuō* (which

---

[146] New Data Show Millions of Americans with Alcohol and Drug Addiction Could Benefit from Health Care R, Partnership for Drug-Free Kids, Sept. 28, 2010.

[147] Jayson, Sharon, *USA Today*, "*More Than 50 Percent of College Students Felt Suicidal*," *ABC News*, Aug. 18, 2008.

[148] Shah, Anup. "*Poverty Facts and Stats*" Global Issues, Jan. 7, 2013.

---

is where we get the word *therapy*) and is defined as "to heal, cure, restore to health."[149]

If we are serious about being disciples and disciple makers, we must become serious about bringing therapy — treating, curing, and restoring those in our hurting world. I learned this firsthand when I struggled with depression.

## Breaking Point

The situation finally came to a breaking point when Connie informed me that I needed to meet with the teachers of our ChildHope School.[150] It was one more request than I could handle. I told Connie, "I cannot go on like this!" "We'll figure this out together," she said. "You will get well." Then she laid her hands on me and started praying for my complete healing. As she prayed, I realized that she had more faith that I'd be healed than I did. Her words of concern were therapeutic in themselves. They served as a soothing balm of hope and understanding I hadn't expected, but desperately needed. In fact, I truly believe that her words put me on the road to healing.

Dismiss any visions of faith healers once found in arenas or in the movies. (Although I have seen many and have personally been healed in such gatherings). God is asking us to be authentic, filled with faith, and bold in our prayers. He wants us to lay hands on the sick and believe that our prayers will be answered and the afflicted will be healed.

When healings happen, faith increases, and some become followers of Jesus Christ. For me, the faith of my wife that I

---

149 Greek Lexicon. G2323 (KJV), *Blue Letter Bible.*
150 www.childhopeonline.org

could be <u>healed</u> gave me faith to believe the same. For the past 10 years, I've been depression free. To God be all the glory!

Raised in a Roman Catholic home, I became quite familiar with what is called the Prayer of Saint Francis of Assisi. One portion of this prayer has become a core principle and technique of our discipleship endeavors: "O divine Master, grant that I may not so much seek ... to be understood, as to understand."

Will we take the time to understand, ask questions, express interest, invest time, and possess the faith to believe that God can truly <u>heal</u> the sick?

Think of the good Samaritan. He not only stops to help a stranger, he offers hope through providing care: "A Samaritan, as he traveled, came where the man was; and when he saw him, he took pity on him. He went to him and bandaged his wounds, pouring on oil and wine" (Luke 10:33,34).

Did you notice that the Samaritan *went to him* and bandaged his wounds? He physically and emotionally touched the man at his point of need and pain. The good Samaritan signifies God's love incarnate.

Leo Tolstoy drove that point home in his book *The Awakening: The Resurrection*. "The whole trouble lies in that people think that there are conditions excluding the necessity of love in their intercourse with man, but such conditions do not exist. Things may be treated without love; one may chop wood, make bricks, forge iron without love, but one can no more deal with people without love than one can handle bees without care."[151]

---

[151] Tolstoy, Graf Leo (2009-10-04). *The Awakening: The Resurrection* (p. 366).

---

## Don't Touch

Alas, the word touch has taken on a street meaning of grope, or the act of groping, or an instance of groping. But touch, when defined as "to cause or permit a part of the body, especially the hand or fingers, to come in contact with so as to feel[152], is a beautiful expression of love, concern, and acceptance.

"But Jesus answered, 'No more of this!' And He touched the man's ear and <u>healed</u> him."[153] The act of appropriate touch is a wanted and needed experience.

The October 2014 issue of *Christianity Today* brought to light this basic need: "Touch is an essential human need. When we shake hands or put an arm across a friend's shoulder, the body releases neurological chemicals like oxytocin and serotonin that feel good, while also inhibiting chemicals that cause stress. But touch doesn't just feel good; it is vital to being human."[154]

The good Samaritan then carries the burden of another person for no other reason than to carry another person's burden.

"Then he put the man on his own donkey, brought him to an inn and took care of him."[155] It's not like the Samaritan had two donkeys. He had only one. We might be willing to give something away if we have a spare.

---

Public Domain Books.
[152] The Free Dictionary.
[153] Luke 22:51.
[154] Moll, Rob. *The Spiritual Power of The Physical Touch*,. Christianity Today, October 2014.
[155] Luke 10:34.

---

You might hear, for example, "Hey, we received two turkeys from our employer; let's give one to the neighbor." But we rarely hear, "Hey, we have one small turkey for Thanksgiving; let's give it to the neighbor."

Beyond caring for a stranger, the good Samaritan also makes a commitment to help another person no matter the cost.

"The next day he took out two denarii and gave them to the innkeeper. 'Look after him,' he said, 'and when I return, I will reimburse you for any extra expense you may have.'"[156] Jesus sums up the entire story with four simple words that give us our marching orders as we make disciples: "Go and do likewise."[157]

## ChildHope

One of our mission's 'likewise' efforts is called ChildHope.[158] The Mission of ChildHope since 1963 is "the transformation of children by means of a relationship with Jesus Christ through a quality education and other ministries of compassion."[159]

ChildHope represents the largest network of Evangelical Christian Schools in Latin America, with 300 schools in 21 countries affecting the lives of more than 100,000 children each day. And more than a million children have attended ChildHope schools. For many children the meal they receive in the school is the only meal they eat each day. Connie and I are proud to participate in such a great 'healing' program.

---

[156] Luke 10:35.
[157] Luke 10:37.
[158] www.childhopeonline.org
[159] Ibid.

## Every Believer Is Empowered to Heal the Sick

Every person, in every age, in every land, who has faith in the living, eternal, covenant-keeping God is empowered to lay hands upon the sick, and "they shall recover" (Mark 16:18).

The general terms of this great extension of the ministry of healing are found in the commission given in Matthew 28: "And Jesus came and spake unto them, saying, all power is given unto me in heaven and in earth" (verse 18). Beloved, has He lost any of that power? Never! He is still the Son of God.[160]

Without a doubt, you know by now that I am a firm believer in healing — present day, divine intervention miracles. One might say, *Well, you believe that because you have never needed a real miracle of healing.* Please understand, Connie and I, as most of you, have struggled with facing unsurmountable life and death situations. And we *did not* see direct and divine intervention. However, burying two of our infants did not destroy our faith in the love, grace, mercy, and healing of our Heavenly Father. Oh, we did have, and still have many questions. Not full-blown doubts really, but questions with no foreseeable answers. But I guess we have come to see that God is so much bigger than our questions, or our doubts.

God is, in other words, so much bigger than our theology. He is before it, around it, at the end of it, and over it. Speaking and thinking about God can be daunting indeed.[161]

We did come to understand that all of life ends in perfect eternal healing and that His grace is sufficient in every dark

---

[160] Lake, J. G. *Divine Healing*. Dutch Church Hall, Somerset East, October 1910.
[161] Morgan, Christopher W. (2010-06-09). *The Glory of God (Theology in Community series)* p. 24. Crossway.

---

situation that the world and Satan has to throw at us. So, lay your doubts and questions behind you and seek to <u>heal</u> the sick and broken.

One of our greatest miracles took place some three years after the death of our babies. Connie continued to struggle with the truth that her dreams had been yanked out of her loving arms.

Her hands and heart ached to care and nurture the children she carried for nine months. And now, because of surgical ligation, she never could give birth again.

After returning to our home church in Louisville, Kentucky, to serve as associate pastors, we became reacquainted with dear friends and fellow members Ray and Betty. Ray and Betty had lost an adolescent son struck by a car in front of their home. And week after week, Betty, knowing that Connie struggled emotionally with the loss of her own children, took her by the hand, gave hugs of support, shared tears of empathy, and whispered words of faith, hope, and love. "Connie, one day you will be happy again," Betty said. "Connie dear, you will hold your children again. This is just one chapter of your life, not the last chapter."

And over several months, Connie did regain wholeness. And then, with the birth of our fourth child[162], she experienced exceedingly abundantly more than she could ask or think.[163]

---

[162] If you are following our story line you will note that after the death of our children, Connie opted for a tubal ligation. But now, a fourth child arrives on the scene! This is not a typo but an incredible answer from a most merciful God. You can find that story in my book, <u>Change – Count on It</u>.

[163] Ephesians 3:20, 21.

The reason I share this story is to reaffirm that we can believe in supernatural healing, even after terrible losses. Sometimes that healing comes through the body of Christ, whose members are sent to heal. And sometimes that healing comes over a period of time.

We are called to heal — through laying on of hands, by listening, a trip to the doctor, a loan of a donkey. We must practice the gift of healing. That is part of the *journey* to which we are called, according to Jesus' instructions in Luke 10:9, "Heal the sick who are there."

You might be one who is not inclined to anoint with oil and lay hands on the sick. (I would encourage all of us to be comfortable with that discipline.) We all, however, have the power of touch and the power of presence. As Betty, like the Samaritan, poured oil and took time with the suffering, Connie found healing. Touch and presence are powerfully miraculous in the hands of His disciples on the *journey*.

Tiffany Field, director of the Touch Research Institute at the University of Miami, and author of the book *Touch*, explains that cultures and families with much physical touch show lower indices of physical aggression. And, even more surprisingly, she writes that the lack of appropriate and healthy touching is why sexual promiscuity and teenage pregnancy are on the increase, and could even explain the increasing incidence of eating disorders and addictive behaviors.

Sadly, the lack of physical contact, Field says, is apparently the cause of increasing isolation or anomie — the sense of normlessness — leading to depression, suicide, and a lack of social cohesion.

## Chronic Loneliness

Much like the subject of touch, social connection is essential for humans' well-being. Long-term loneliness can be lethal. Sorrowfully, more people report chronic loneliness compared to 20 years ago, and this in turn may contribute to the rising death toll in the U.S.[164]

> "Humans were not designed to be solitary creatures," says Laura Entis, *Fortune* associate editor. "We evolved to survive in tribes; the need to interact is deeply ingrained in our genetic code. So much so, that the absence of social connection triggers the same, primal alarm bells as hunger, thirst, and physical pain."[165]

## Perilous **Healers**

Verdant walls overflowing with jungle flora flanked both sides. No doubt those walls also brimmed with stinging insects, exotic animals, and poisonous snakes. With each step, they move ever closer to an ambitious goal — to reach an Amazonian tribe at the northeastern tip of Ecuador with the message of Christ's love and grace. It's a lofty pursuit because no outsider has ever survived first contact with the nomadic nation.

Nylon packs are strapped to their backs. Each pack contains a few energy bars, ready-to-eat meals, a first-aid kit, a knife,

---

[164] Cacioppo, John. *Loneliness: Human Nature and the Need for Social Connection.* (p. 8) W. W. Norton & Co.
[165] Entis, Laura. (2016-06-22) *Chronic Loneliness Is a Modern-Day Epidemic.* *Fortune* magazine.

---

some rope, a personalized water-filtration system, and soap — 40 pounds of soap. That soap is their key. They use it to gain entrance into each primitive tribal community they encounter.

Their treks are perilous, but they press forward, despite my words of warning and concern. It's not that I'd ever ask them to stop; that would be foolish. They are my kids, and I know what it is to carry a vision that is beyond oneself, as I too have obeyed the command to go despite the fair warnings of others.

My kids — Joil (my son-in-law), Leah (my daughter), Seth (my son), and Kaitlin (my daughter-in-law) — are kneeling on the banks of a slow-moving, brown river with the chief of a small village kneeling beside them. In their hands they each hold a bar of soap. Like well-trained hawkers, they extol its cleaning powers and health benefits as if they were on QVC.

The chief nods as they take great pains to point out that if the tribal people use soap regularly, they'll not only combat disease and sickness, but the infant mortality rate in the village will drop dramatically. The chief raises his eyebrows, and our kids are positive they have his undivided attention.

In an instant, they skillfully transition the conversation to stories about Jesus and how He can wash away the sins of the chief and his people.

"This is of great benefit," Leah says as the chief nods.

This is how my kids are going, how they are making disciples. They are taking treks through the Amazon with little money, food, or supplies. They are healers, making friends with indigenous people who have had little contact with outsiders. They are giving gifts of soap. They are talking about Jesus while facing the very real risk they could be killed for their outreach efforts. Each trek they take is a perilous, but fantastic *journey* of healing.

They wouldn't have it any other way.

Regardless of the method we employ — soap, schools, listening or laying on of hands in Jesus' name — we are called to heal. The Scripture's promise of healing stands today as unwavering as the day the prophet wrote, "He was pierced for our transgressions, He was crushed for our iniquities; the punishment that brought us peace was on Him, and by His wounds we are healed" (Isaiah 53:5).

And directly from the hymnal of the Old Testament, Israel sang the words of David: "Praise the LORD, my soul; all my inmost being, praise His holy name. Praise the LORD, my soul, and forget not all His benefits—who forgives all your sins and heals all your diseases" (Psalm 103:1-3).

Once we go forth to heal we will then find opportunities to *tell*. Word thirteen is coming up.

# S.T.O.P.

**Consider again the word <u>Heal</u> and ask yourself the following questions:**

What was Jesus conveying to His disciples by giving them this command?

What did Jesus want them to understand?

What does the word <u>Heal</u> now mean to me?

What does Jesus want to convey to me through this word?

**Now let's live it out. How will you respond to what you have heard, read, learned, or felt inspired to do?**

S. SPECIFIC: What specifically will you do in response to the key word <u>Heal</u>?

T. TIME-SENSITIVE: Within what time frame will you begin or complete the task?

O. OBTAINABLE: Is it possible? If not, go back to S.

P. PERTINENT: How does this goal relate to the key word and our understanding of it?

*Read It - Think It - Write It - Share It*

180

# 13

## Word Thirteen – Tell
### *Practical Proclamation*

Key word: Tell – To speak out, speak of, mention[166]

Key verse: "…tell them, 'The kingdom of God has come near to you'" (Luke 10:9).

Key thought: The sharing of one's testimony of coming to faith in Jesus is the greatest sermon a person will ever preach.

———————

Eduardo sat across the table from me. His eyes were heavy. Frustration furrowed his brow as pensive lines etched his face. He talked about his regrets, despair, frustrations, and fears. We'd had many deep talks, but I'd never seen him like this before, so I listened intently to every word he said. He needed to pull the splinters from his soul.

*"I'm on the verge of losing everything,"* he said stoically. *"I've lost my way."*

I nodded understandingly, then offered, *"I can't help you, Eduardo."*

He immediately shook his head from side to side in disgust, to which I quickly replied, *"But I know Who can."*

———————————————

166 Greek Lexicon. G3004 (KJV), *Blue Letter Bible.*

———

He pulled a pen from his coat pocket. *"I want this man's number. I will call him and set a meeting immediately. If you can't help, maybe he can."*

I smiled. "That won't be necessary."

*"And why not?"*

*"Because you can talk to Him right now,"* I said. *"I'm talking about Jesus."*

As I pointed toward heaven, Eduardo leaned back and sighed. *"Jesus? Really?"*

*"Yes,"* I said, leaning in to be sure I had his full attention. *"May I tell you a story?"*

He nodded. *"Absolutely."*

I waded into a story — my story. I told of the days before I had committed my life to Jesus. I told of how in Jesus I found peace, healing, and a purpose for existing. I told Eduardo that Jesus met me when I, too, couldn't seem to find the answers.

"Let the redeemed of the Lord tell their story — those he redeemed from the hand of the foe" (Psalm 107:2).

## Preach

When I use the word *preach,* what immediately comes to mind? Probably an individual standing before a crowd sharing the points of a biblical message. Preaching runs the gamut from an animated orator behind a pulpit to something that resembles a TED Talk[167] type of presentation.

Most definitely there are times and places where preaching is delivered from a platform, stage or boat, in a theater, amphitheater, or assembly hall. Jesus used all these on occasion, as did Peter, Paul, Stephen, and others.

My concern is that this picture of preaching is practically the only image that comes to mind when we use the word preach. Allow me to give you a replacement word to better convey the entire scope of the term. Every time you hear the word *preach*, attach the word *proclaim* or *tell* to your understanding. Preaching might include what is done from a stage or pulpit (interestingly the word *pulpit* comes from the word *stage*), or someone at a bus stop talking with a friend. Look at the following verses to see how the same Greek word is translated into English.

*Preach* – Mark 16:15. "He said to them, 'Go into all the world and *preach* the gospel to all creation.'"

*Proclaim* – Matthew 10:7. "As you go, *proclaim* this message: 'The kingdom of heaven has come near.'"

*Tell* – Mark 5:20. "So the man went away and began to *tell* in the Decapolis how much Jesus had done for him. And all the people were amazed."

I like how the NIV uses the word *tell* in Mark 5:20 and also Luke 10:9. It sounds a little softer and is applicable to all

---

[167] TED is a nonpartisan nonprofit devoted to spreading ideas, usually in the form of short, powerful talks. TED began in 1984 as a conference where Technology, Entertainment and Design converged, and today covers almost all topics — from science to business to global issues — in more than 110 languages. *https://www.ted.com/*

followers of Jesus. But that brings us to the rub. Somehow we have turned the practice of preaching into an office of the church. We call our pastors *preachers* and say such people are "called to preach." This is more than semantics. Yes, we have people called to offices in the body of Christ: pastors, teachers, and apostles, for example. But preaching, first of all, is not an office. Secondly, everyone is called to <u>tell</u> the story.

You might wonder why I am getting so picky. Glad you asked. I have four main reasons:

1.  When the preaching of the Word is relegated to the "called" or to a clergy class, we eliminate about 99 percent of our workforce from the responsibility of telling the story.

2.  When we elevate the pulpit to "altar" status, we put it out of reach for most believers, and damage the powerful and important tool of <u>telling</u>.

3.  Most of our congregations won't measure up to the standards, gifting, and talents of "preacher," yet Jesus expects everyone to proclaim.

4.  We damage the true definition of what it means to preach.

Everyone can <u>tell</u> a powerful story, and I mean everyone. The reason? We can be great storytellers if we stick to the accounts we know best — our own stories.

Our call to preach, teach, proclaim, prophesy, or <u>tell</u>, is not to better educate the lost. The purpose of our proclaiming is to move our listener, observer, or reader to discipleship, thereby glorifying God in the life of the new believer (Romans 12: 2; James 1: 22).

## Storytelling

Jesus modeled the art of storytelling for us. A few elements of His storytelling prowess should be emulated. For instance, He knew His audiences. He knew what stories would make sense to them. He knew how to draw comparisons that would get them thinking. And He knew how to break down the complexities of theology so that it would be attainable for everyone He met, including children.

You're probably thinking, *Great. I have to be a renowned preacher to be a great and powerful storyteller.* That's not true. All you have to do is <u>tell</u> your story and stick with it; the Holy Spirit will take care of the rest. That's why we can have confidence when we <u>tell</u> our listeners, "The kingdom of God has come near to you."[168]

Wanda is Connie's cousin, and when we began to date, Connie was Wanda's go-to baby sitter. I can remember picking up Connie from baby-sitting, and Wanda would always engage me with a testimony of what God was doing in her life. Oh, she was not a perfect individual, but she did have a genuine, sincere and magnetic testimony — a testimony that brought Christ and the Scriptures to life. Wanda's story of faith caused me to see a living resurrection of Jesus.

Storytelling is one of the most powerful weapons in the arsenal of the Church. Chronicles of the redeemed — shrouded in love — transform our lives one at a time.

> "The history of mankind is crowded with evidences proving that physical coercion is not adapted to moral regeneration," writes Leo Tolstoy. "and that the sinful dispositions of men can be subdued only by love; that evil can be exterminated only by good; that

---

[168] Luke 10:9.

---

185

it is not safe to rely upon the strength of an arm to preserve us from harm; that there is great security in being gentle, longsuffering, and abundant in mercy; that it is only the meek who shall inherit the earth; for those who take up the sword shall perish by the sword."[169]

## The Apostle's Story

The apostle Paul shares his story in the Book of Acts. His account demonstrates how wonderfully Jesus can transform a life. Like all good stories, Paul's has three basic elements: his past, his conversion, and his current situation.

In Acts 26:9-11, Paul tells King Agrippa about his past. As with all of us, his past is filled with mistakes, regrets, and poor decisions. Though at times it can be difficult to identify with another's success, most everyone can identify with another's failures. In other words, our past failures are powerful tools for relating to other people.

The apostle does not hold back when talking of his failings and errors. "I too was convinced that I ought to do all that was possible to oppose the name of Jesus of Nazareth," he says.

> "And that is just what I did in Jerusalem. On the authority of the chief priests I put many of the Lord's people in prison, and when they were put to death, I cast my vote against them. Many a time I went from one synagogue to another to have them punished, and I tried to force them to blaspheme.

---

[169] Tolstoy, Leo (2011-07-12). *The Kingdom of God Is Within You* (pp. 4-5). Kindle Edition.

I was so obsessed with persecuting them that I even hunted them down in foreign cities."

After telling the story of his past — admitting the sins and failures that marked it — Paul moves on to the moment when the love, grace, and hope of Jesus transformed his life. In many ways, this is an excellent teaching moment, as it provides a follower of Christ an opportunity to share the path of salvation.

"On one of these *journeys* I was going to Damascus with the authority and commission of the chief priests," Paul continues. "About noon, King Agrippa, as I was on the road, I saw a light from heaven, brighter than the sun, blazing around me and my companions. We all fell to the ground, and I heard a voice saying to me in Aramaic, 'Saul, Saul, why do you persecute me? It is hard for you to kick against the goads.'

"Then I asked, 'Who are you, Lord?'

"'I am Jesus, whom you are persecuting,' the Lord replied. 'Now get up and stand on your feet. I have appeared to you to appoint you as a servant and as a witness of what you have seen and will see of Me. I will rescue you from your own people and from the Gentiles. I am sending you to them to open their eyes and turn them from darkness to light, and from the power of Satan to God, so that they may receive forgiveness of sins and a place among those who are sanctified by faith in Me'" (Acts 26:12-18).

After sharing his history and about the moment he committed his life to Jesus, Paul brings his present circumstances into context by sharing the hope he has. In doing so, Paul tells how his faith has transformed his life in a personal and lasting way.

> "So then, King Agrippa, I was not disobedient to the vision from heaven," the apostle goes on. "First to those in Damascus, then to those in Jerusalem and in all Judea, and then to the Gentiles, I preached that they should repent and turn to God and demonstrate their repentance by their deeds. That is why some Jews seized me in the temple courts and tried to kill me. But God has helped me to this very day; so I stand here and testify to small and great alike."[170]

Paul's story is powerful. And so is yours! Think about it. Cynics and doubters can argue the existence of God and the validity of religion in today's culture, but it's hard to argue with how someone feels or how his or her life has been transformed by Jesus.

In church, people call your story a testimony. No matter how you describe it, your story goes beyond the doctrine of a church, the failures of church leaders, the popular political positions of the day, or whether religion is viable in today's culture. Your story is a testament to your relationship with Jesus. The key word in that last sentence is *relationship*.

One's faith in Christ and one's testimony of faith is powerful enough to overcome all the works of evil. The apostle John makes that clear when he tells followers of Jesus that they can overcome the enemy of their faith "by the blood of the Lamb and by the word of their testimony."[171]

---

[170] Acts 26:19-22.
[171] Revelation 12:11, NKJV.

Undoubtedly, Paul had shared his testimony of coming to faith many times before. He was prepared at a moment's notice to share his life-transforming encounter with Jesus. In the same way, I encourage my disciples to know their testimony and to be ready to share their story whenever the opportunity arises.

I was able to encourage one such believer in the first church Connie and I pastored in Kentucky. Jean took the challenge and wrote her story, *A Jehovah's Witness Finds the Truth*. It's Jean's story of coming to a personal encounter with Jesus after studying her way out of a third-generation commitment to the Watchtower organization. Obviously, Jean fashioned her story well, and countless seekers have found a new *journey* through her testimony.[172]

The practice of crafting one's story is critical to going and making disciples. I believe that every follower of Jesus should be able to <u>tell</u> his or her story in three minutes or less. The elements of the story should include the past, conversion, and present elements, just like Paul's testimony. I also recommend that before you share your story with someone else, you rehearse it by sharing it with loved ones. The reason? If you follow Jesus' command to go and make disciples, you're going to have ample opportunity to share your story.[173] After all, God already has placed a person of peace in your path. Let's make sure we are ready to proclaim our testimony when opportunities avail.

---

[172] Eason, Jean. *A Jehovah's Witness Finds the Truth (Revised Edition)*. Love Agape Ministries Press, 1999. Jean's Book can be read for free: www.tutorsforchrist.org

[173] At the close of this chapter, a worksheet prepared by CRU (formerly Campus Crusade for Christ) will help you write your own unique story of redemption.

I shared my story with Eduardo. He challenged a few points of my testimony as he struggled to wrap his mind — and, more importantly, his soul — around the truth I shared with him.

In the following months, he and I met on a regular basis. During those talks I filled in the blanks, reminded him of the low points before I knew Jesus, and the highlights of when I found Jesus. We met every Wednesday evening and talked late into the night. In doing so, we read Scriptures, shared our experiences, and prayed together. That's what making disciples looks like. It's nothing too complicated, but it must be authentic and intentional.

As we walked in discipleship, I fleshed out all the angles of my story and answered Eduardo's questions. When I didn't have an answer, I simply replied, "I don't know" or "I will need to get back to you on that one." A testimony of one's own powerful encounter with Christ can withstand the difficult and impossible questions. By being vigilant and dedicated to making a disciple of Eduardo, I knew it was only a matter of time before the Holy Spirit seized his heart and mind and led him to Jesus. That is not confidence in myself, but rather confidence in the power of the Holy Spirit.

Eduardo eventually committed his life to Jesus and has dedicated himself to going and making disciples. He and his wife Ximena continue to powerfully impact their culture today. Their stories are a reflection of a discipleship *journey*.

"...until we all reach unity in the faith and in the knowledge of the Son of God and become mature, attaining to the whole measure of the fullness of Christ."[174]

---

[174] Ephesians 4:13.

# S.T.O.P.

**Consider the key word again and ask yourself the following questions:**

What was Jesus conveying to His disciples when he calls on us to <u>Tell</u>?

What did Jesus want them to understand thought this command?

What does the word <u>Tell</u> now mean to me?

What does Jesus want to convey to me through this word?

**Now let's live it out. How will you respond to what you have heard, read, learned, or felt inspired to do?**

S. SPECIFIC: What specifically will you do in response to the key word <u>Tell</u>?

T. TIME-SENSITIVE: Within what time frame will you begin or complete the task?

O. OBTAINABLE: Is it possible? If not, go back to S.

P. PERTINENT: How does this goal relate to the key word and our understanding of it?

*Read It - Think It - Write It - Share It*

191

# Conclusion

Well, there we have it — 13 words of Jesus that, when properly applied, will revolutionize our *journey* of being and making disciples. These are not 13 sequential steps, not keys to a quick fix or shortcut, but 13 landing stages to a solid path of fruitful living.

Let's look at The *Journey* again as a checklist, to be sure I have adequately explained the process.

## 1. Appointed – Prevailing Purpose

The *journey*, as a disciple of Christ, is a call and appointment to serve specifically within the body of Christ. We should strive to decipher and exercise that gift. The overarching call, however, is to bring glory to God. The *journey* is all about His glory, which gives us a prevailing purpose.

## 2. Two – Community Caravan

The micro and macro calls are fulfilled through living in community. And that community should be on the move. It's a lot like a caravan of believers, a Community Caravan.

## 3. Ask – Poignant Petition

Words 1 and 2, Appointed and Two, call for mental, spiritual and emotional preparations for the *journey*. Word 3, however, is a call to action, a call to ask poignantly.

## 4. Go – Motivated Movement

The word *journey* conveys the idea of movement. Like gears in a clock, some move quickly, others move in reverse, and a few are nearly motionless, yet all are moving for the same purpose and in perfect harmony. With the word Go, Jesus is motivating His disciples' movement.

### 5. Wolves – Appreciated Anguish

Anguish and pain are imbedded in the *journey* of faith. Not pain for pain's sake — it's just an inevitable part of the process. A part that we can eventually appreciate.

### 6. Purse – Cashless Capital

Some activities are priceless, some can be cashless, and the *journey* is made up of both. Some of the most effective work of the Kingdom needs no cash, but a lot of capital.

### 7. Sandals – Sticky Stops

The *journey* is about finding places where we can stop long enough to gather others for the trip. Hopefully, throughout the *journey*, we will find places to stop where the gospel will stick, sticky stops.

### 8. Greet – Disastrous Distractions

The best of plans, initiatives and inspirations will fall under the weight of disastrous distractions.

### 9. Enter – Daunting Doors

It's one thing to arrive at a destination, it's quite another to be personally invited to enter beyond the door of one's place of security and comfort. Unfamiliar doors in unknown places can be quite daunting.

### 10. Peace – Likeable Links

People of Peace are individuals with whom you "click" in a healthy manner. They become the links, likeable links to bring the gospel to entire families and communities. Jesus calls His disciples to nurture such connections.

### 11. Eat – Meaningful Meals

One of the very best opportunities for discipleship is found during a shared meal. Jesus knows that to eat and share a meal with another requires a minimum level of trust that can lead to <u>meaningful</u> relationships, which can be a crucial key to spiritual transformation.

### 12. Heal – Therapeutic Theology
All people hurt, struggle, suffer, or are wounded — *everyone*. We all need healing, and Jesus calls us to do just that, <u>heal</u>. The <u>theology</u> of the *journey* is one that must be <u>therapeutic</u>.

### 13. Tell – Practical Proclamation
The sharing of one's testimony of coming to faith in Jesus is the greatest sermon a person will ever preach. It is a <u>practical proclamation </u>of the Good News.

Enjoy your *journey*!

*Appendix A*

# Questionnaire Checklist

## Appointed – Prevailing Purpose
Do I understand that my purpose for the *journey* is to bring glory to God, that is, that He would be revealed through me as I *journey* through life?

## Two – Community Caravan
Remember, this cannot be done alone. Am I actively participating in a healthy community of believers that are encouraging me on the *journey*?

## Ask – Poignant Petition
Jesus bids me to ask in prayer for workers and to pray for others. Am I actively asking in prayer — for me and for others — for the Lord to send workers?

## Go – Motivated Movement
A stagnant *journey* is no *journey* at all. Can I see that I am making progress? Is my life a source of faith for others?

## Wolves – Appreciated Anguish
What are the wolves in my path? Are they inhibiting my *journey*? How should I deal with them?

## Purse – Cashless Capital
What can I do today to advance the gospel without spending a penny? Am I building a capital of faith? How?

## Sandals – Sticky Stops
Am I moving with purpose? Are there places along this *journey*'s path where I need to stop and allow my faith to impact those around me?

———

**Greet – Disastrous Distractions**
Have I lost focus? What is the *journey* all about? What are the distractions that might be pulling me off the *journey*'s path?

**Enter – Daunting Doors**
When was the last time I was invited beyond the front door of someone's home or even life? Did I take advantage of the invitation?

**Peace – Likeable Links**
Are there some people of peace in my life? Would, should these be opportunities to heal and share my testimony of coming to faith?

**Eat – Meaningful Meals**
Are my meals meaningful events? How can my meal times be better used for good? How can we grow through eating together?

**Heal – Therapeutic Theology**
Do I see those around me as needing healing? Am I always looking to be healed, or am I looking to heal? What can I do today to ease someone's pain?

**Tell – Practical Proclamation**
Do I understand that my testimony is my most powerful tool in proclaiming the Kingdom? Can I share my past, my story of salvation and how it has changed my life, all within a few minutes? Have I done it?

*Appendix B*

# Your Testimony
## How to Prepare and Tell Your Story
### By CRU [175]

Take a few minutes now, working through these questions, and be ready for the next open-door God gives you to tell your story.

**Before I Accepted Christ
(or gave Him complete control)**

1. What was my life like that will relate most to the non-Christian?

2. What did my life revolve around the most? What did I get my security or happiness from? (The non-Christian is relying on something external to give him happiness)

3. How did those areas begin to let me down?

**How I Received Christ
(or gave Him complete control)**

1. When was the first time I heard the gospel? (Or when was I exposed to dynamic Christianity?)

2. What were my initial reactions?

---

[175] By Permission: Cru is the name of Campus Crusade for Christ in the United States. Cru is an interdenominational Christian evangelism and discipleship ministry. For more information, visit **www.cru.org**.

3. When did my attitude begin to turn around? Why?

4. What were the final struggles that went through my mind just before I accepted Christ?

5. Why did I go ahead and accept Christ?

**After I Accepted Christ
(or gave Him complete control)**

1. Specific changes and illustrations about the changes Christ has made:

2. Why am I motivated differently?

**Helpful Hints**

1. Write the way you speak; make the testimony yours.

2. Practice this over and over until it becomes natural.

3. Shoot for short – three minutes. At that length, it's easily something you can put into a conversation without it becoming a monologue.

*Appendix C*

# A Word About Mentoring

*By Frankie Powell*

I must confess that I only had two personal mentors in my life. That's not to say that I was not constantly mentored throughout my life by great people, but most of it was through books, cassette tapes, CDs and videos. Still today, through mp3s and books, I continue to gain wisdom and insight that I need, from many examples, to continue my *journey* of mentoring.

I've had the privilege of mentoring several young people in my life. In the beginning, I did not think of it as mentoring, neither did I have a specific plan or strategy as such, nor could I have put it into words as I can today as I write this annex.

I only knew three things that shaped my *journey* and they were simple things that profoundly impacted my desire to mentor others.

First, the words of Paul to his mentee Timothy found in 2 Timothy 2:1-2; "You then, my son, be strong in the grace that is in Christ Jesus. And the things you have heard me say in the presence of many witnesses entrust to reliable people who will also be qualified to teach others."

These words marked my life in my early twenties and I knew I wanted to impact the lives of others, even those I would never know personally. Though I didn't understand this then or could have it explained it as I will now, nevertheless, it was a burning desire. Today I would call it legacy, and I would tell you that my mission in life is to make a difference in the lives of those who want to make a difference in the lives of others.

Second, and perhaps the greatest impact on my desire to mentor others comes from the biblical story of Elisha, found in 1 and 2 Kings. He was Elijah's protégé and he received a "double portion" of Elijah's spirit or life, when Elijah left this earth. Great story and very true though often misapplied. I'll save that for another time and place.

Elisha lived a great and successful life and then he died. He was buried in a cave. And the story continues in 2 Kings 13:21; "Once while some Israelites were burying a man, suddenly they saw a band of raiders; so they threw the man's body into Elisha's tomb. When the body touched Elisha's bones, the man came to life and stood up on his feet." And the church said, amen.

Not so fast. This verse said to me that Elisha had received *from* his mentor but never mentored anyone else, so all of his life experiences died with him. The impact it made on me was that I want to die empty! I want to pour my life into the lives of others, as Elijah did, so that when I leave this life, I have been a good steward of all God has allowed me to experience.

The third and final principle that impacted my desire to mentor others comes from Psalm 127:4; "Like arrows in the hands of a warrior are children born in one's youth."

Though there is much to be said about our natural children, it said to me that I should do all I can to launch those I mentor, by sharing my experiences — good and bad — dos and don'ts, successes and failures, in such a way that they will be able to take what I have taught them and accomplish so much more than I ever could and so much faster than I ever will.

So, my strategy for mentoring is simple, yet intentional. I live with a hunger to be and do all God has planned for my life and during the process of pursuing, finding, failing, and fulfilling my purpose, and it is a never-ending process, I share my practices, principles, and pitfalls with those I am mentoring.

Here is what it looks like. We spend much time walking out life and ministry together. We read books and discuss them. We have a daily Bible reading plan in which we discuss the Scriptures and apply them to everyday life on a regular basis. We memorize portions of Scripture while making personal applications as we go. We spend a lot of time asking and answering questions of each other, and no subject is off limits. We learn about missions, finances, family, as well as leadership, self-awareness, and relationships. We pray together regularly, and times of fasting are a definite part of this relationship.

This kind of mentorship takes a tremendous amount of humility. And like Bill, I have often struggled with being PROUD of my humility. It's the never-ending process. It requires authenticity and a lot of discipline, including spiritual disciplines, because you cannot give to others something you do not have yourself. We do not reproduce what we say or do, we reproduce who we are, plain and simple.

This style of mentoring doesn't happen in a classroom or meeting. It happens in life, it is very time consuming, and it must be adamantly intentional.

In closing, let me say I have probably failed at this more than I have succeeded, but the reward that makes it worthwhile is to see those whom I have mentored become mighty men and women of God. And the truest satisfaction comes with knowing, wherever they go, whatever they accomplish, and whoever they become for the sake of Christ, I played a small part in helping them reach their potential and fulfill their purpose in the earth. Selah.

Frankie Powell<br>
Pastor/Evangelist<br>
frankie@frankiepowell.com

# Acknowledgements

If this book has been of any inspiration, direction or encouragement, please know that the following individuals played a huge part in making it happen.

Connie McDonald
Kirk Noonan
John Kennedy
Joil Marbut
Allen Kidd
Jean Eason
José and Melissa Pabón
Betty Thompson Owens
Joe Girdler
Mark Lehmann
Frankie Powell
Bob and Mary Burton

"Your love has given me great joy and encouragement, because you, *brothers and sisters*, have refreshed the hearts of the Lord's people" (Philemon 1:7).

***Thank you!***

# Contact Us

I want to thank you for taking time to read this small volume. My heart's desire is that the message of Jesus and the Father's grace might find new rich soil for where it may grow in abundance. If we can be of any further assistance, please feel free to contact us through the information below.

**Seminars and Speaking** – Connie and I would be most honored to bring *The Journey* seminar or message to your congregation or group. Please contact us for additional information and scheduling.

**Church Planting** – We are also available to coach church planters in *The Journey* process in person, online or through video conferencing. Additional information is available upon request.

**Television** – We invite you to follow our growing television and IPTV channels. See the links below.

**This book is also available in Spanish.**

**Other contact information:**
Facebook – @pastorbillmcdonald
Joil & Leah Marbut – www.junglemissionary.com
Unsión Television – www.unsion.tv
Asambleas de Dios Television – www.adtv-online.com

The *Journey*
Bill and Connie McDonald
P.O. 98
Crestwood, KY 40014

76727055R00125

Made in the USA
Middletown, DE
15 June 2018